W9-ATD-379

LEGENDS

THE BEST PLAYERS, GAMES, AND TEAMS IN

BASKETBALL

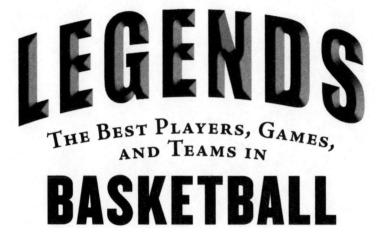

LEGENDS

The Best Players, Games, and Teams in

BASKETBALL

HOWARD BRYANT

PHILOMEL BOOKS

Also by Howard Bryant

Legends: The Best Players, Games, and Teams in Baseball
Legends: The Best Players, Games, and Teams in Football

PHILOMEL BOOKS
an imprint of Penguin Random House LLC
375 Hudson Street
New York, NY 10014

Copyright © 2017 by Howard Bryant.

Library of Congress Cataloging-in-Publication Data is available upon request.
Printed in the United States of America.
ISBN 9780399169052
1 3 5 7 9 10 8 6 4 2

Edited by Michael Green.
Design by Semadar Megged.
Text set in 12.5/19-point Apollo MT Std.

Dedicated to Christopher Sauceda,
and his lifelong love of basketball

CONTENTS

The 2010s

A Note from Howard Bryant

When I was a kid, I dreamed of what I would be when I got older. Starting around third grade, I wanted to be a cartoonist. In class, when I was supposed to be paying attention to my teacher, I would draw superheroes instead. I collected comics (Marvel Comics only! Sorry, Batman and Superman.) for the adventure, but also to practice drawing Thor and Loki, Nightcrawler from the X-Men, and of course, Daredevil, the Man Without Fear.

Later on, I wanted to be an astronomer. I loved the solar system and knew every fact about each planet: its size, density, surface, and number of moons. (Back then, Jupiter had sixteen known moons. Now it has sixty-seven!)

The world was open and free. Anything was possible.

And then, starting in seventh grade, like a

Category 5 hurricane reaching the mainland, basketball arrived—and wiped out everything that had ever existed before.

Drawing? Adios. All I cared about was making sure I could dribble as well with my left hand as I could with my right, like the all-time great point guard Isiah Thomas could when he first hit the scene as a Detroit Piston. I still read comics, but now *Basketball Digest*, *Basketball Times*, and *Basketball Weekly* arrived in the mail and my new basketball heroes took priority over superheroes.

Astronaut? Forget it. The only star I wanted to see soar was the great Julius Erving, better known as "Dr. J," who was Michael Jordan *before* there was a Michael Jordan. The Celtics were my new solar system. Suddenly, my world revolved around the greats like Larry Bird, Robert Parish, Tiny Archibald, and Dennis Johnson. I didn't fear anything—the flu, bad grades, nuclear war—nearly as much as I feared for the Celtics when they played the dreaded Philadelphia 76ers and soon the even more dreaded Los Angeles Lakers.

The other sports I loved—hockey, baseball, football, and tennis—took a backseat. My love of basketball consumed my waking hours, and I enjoyed playing it just as much as I relished watching the greats in the NBA dazzle fans night after night. People in my neighborhood could hear the basketball I was dribbling before they could see me coming down the street. And I still revere the game today.

This book is about the miracles of the game, of what basketball used to be (no three-point shots, few dunks, and get this—no jump shots!) *and* what it is today in 2017 (Lob City, LeBron James, and the Splash Brothers, Steph Curry and Klay Thompson of the high-octane Golden State Warriors).

Prepare to embark on a journey through the many eras of professional basketball, from the old days, when there were NBA teams in Syracuse, Buffalo, and St. Louis but *none* in Miami, San Antonio, or Dallas; to a time when there were *two* competing leagues, one that played with a red, white, and blue ball; to the 1980s resurgence that brought the world the "Showtime" LA Lakers starring Magic Johnson and their rivalry with Larry Bird's Boston Celtics; to the near-mythical '90s Age of Jordan; to the present, with LeBron and Steph Curry exciting fans today the way Dr. J did for me during my childhood.

Growing up, basketball was the springboard for so many things that would come later: Watching hoops made me want to read more about the history of basketball and all the greats who played before I was born. Reading about basketball made me want to read more about everything else, which created a lifetime love of reading. Reading made me want to write my own sentences and form my own views about what I thought was important on the court and in the world, which produced a love of writing that exists to this day. So even though I never grew another inch past the tenth grade, never became a professional player, and am so bad at drawing now that I can't even draw a smiley face unless it's an emoji, you could say it was all worth it because you could say basketball made me want to be a writer, which is where I was supposed to be all along.

The magic of basketball is powerful enough to be applied to everything. Even if I never had a chance to play on an NBA court, loving the game as I did still got me where I wanted to go in life. And to this day, my love of the game remains as strong as it was the very first day I ever dribbled a basketball.

THE
1960s

THE STORY
OF THE 1960s

THE BOSTON CELTICS

n 1921, the New York Yankees reached the World
Series for the first time. Two years later, they won
their first championship. In the forty-four seasons
between 1921 and 1964, the Yankees appeared in
the World Series twenty-nine times and won twenty
championships. They were simply the best team in
professional sports. Perhaps the closest were hockey's
Montreal Canadiens, who won their sixth Stanley
Cup in 1944 and were really just getting started.
After playing in twenty-four Stanley Cups and winning eighteen times over the next thirty-five years,
the Canadiens achieved legendary status, emerging as

the Yankees of professional hockey (though I'm sure hockey fans consider it the other way around).

In the early days of pro basketball, the NBA had a handful of good teams, like the Syracuse Nationals and St. Louis Hawks, and one great one, the Minneapolis Lakers. The Lakers won five NBA titles between 1949 and 1954, and had the first dominant big man in six-foot-ten George Mikan, a player no defender could guard. But even the Lakers weren't on the level of a team like the Yankees or Canadiens.

No, the first truly great dynasty in the NBA belonged to the Boston Celtics of the 1960s.

It happened the way so many history-changing events do: with someone believing in a dream, and someone else possessing a little luck and a lot more forethought than the rest, the ability to see a tiny bit of the future, and a willingness to take a risk and trust one's instincts.

Walter Brown and Arnold "Red" Auerbach were those people. Brown founded the Celtics in 1945, and here was the thing that is really unbelievable today:

At the time, most people believed basketball would never become popular.

Walter Brown was not one of those people.

Brown believed in basketball so much he risked his house. He sold his furniture to own the Celtics. By the late '50s, Auerbach was already considered a great coach, but up until that point, his teams hadn't been good enough to beat New York or Minneapolis. He had been the coach of the Celtics since the beginning, and by 1956, Auerbach had a team that was improving yet was still missing that winning ingredient that could catapult them into the realm of champions.

Sure, the Celtics could certainly score. They had a wonderfully creative point guard in Bob Cousy, a wizard who could dribble as if he played for the Harlem Globetrotters. Cousy was a star, a point guard who could score and was well known for his fancy no-look passes as well as his ability to dribble out the clock without letting anyone steal the ball from him. Before Bill Russell, Cousy was the face of the Boston Celtics, a fan favorite who had attended Holy Cross, in nearby Worcester, Massachusetts.

Boston had a high-scoring shooting guard named Bill Sharman, and a star center, "Easy" Ed Macauley. Between 1950 and 1956, the Celtics made the playoffs every year but never reached the final round.

After posting a 39-33 record in the 1955–56 regular

season and losing early in the playoffs again, Auerbach knew his team needed a change. They needed to be tougher defensively. They needed to be more active.

They needed Bill Russell.

Bill Russell was the best college player in the country, having led the University of San Francisco to back-to-back college championships. He finished his senior year with a fifty-five-game winning streak. He was six foot nine, could outjump anyone, and was a ferocious competitor.

In those days, the NBA was nothing like today, when LeBron James can dunk from the foul line and Russell Westbrook goes coast-to-coast, rebound-to-dunk, and Steph Curry can shoot and dribble like a genius. Back then, the game was slow. The big guys were tall and strong, but they didn't have the speed or jumping ability of today's big men. Most players still shot the "two-handed set shot," which meant they shot the ball almost like a foul shot, releasing the ball close to chest level rather than above one's head, or the one-hander, where they took the ball in one hand and pushed it to the basket. Try it! Believe it or not, jump shots didn't become a significant part of the game until *years* later.

Bill Russell was the game's first super-athlete. His

vertical leap was 48 inches off the ground. That's FOUR FEET! He literally could jump *four feet off the ground*! Centers back then were expected to score, but they didn't block shots and play defense the way they do today.

While other teams couldn't sense change, Auerbach thought about a new kind of basketball—a faster, more athletic game. Russell was just the guy he needed to make that dream a reality.

There was a problem, though. The Rochester Royals (who are the Sacramento Kings today) held the first pick. Russell didn't want to play in Rochester, so he demanded more money than he thought the Royals would pay. He was right; the Royals selected a shooting guard most people today have never heard of, Sihugo Green. The St. Louis Hawks had the second pick, and here Auerbach saw his chance, offering to trade one of his best players, Macauley, plus forward Cliff Hagan, in exchange for Russell.

So what to do if you're St. Louis? Do you keep Russell, a college and Olympic champion who had never played a minute in the NBA, or trade Russell for Macauley, who had proven he could not only play in the NBA but also be one of its stars?

The decision would be one of the most important in basketball history.

The Hawks chose to trade Russell to Boston.

Auerbach had his man.

With the Celtics' other picks in the draft, Auerbach selected Tom Heinsohn and K. C. Jones, who was one of Russell's teammates at USF. Jones was heading to the army but would return.

In the 1956–57 season, the Celtics' roster included Russell, Sharman, Cousy, Heinsohn, and Frank Ramsey. Incredibly, all five would one day be elected to the pro basketball Hall of Fame.

From the moment they first stepped on the court together, it was clear they were destined for greatness.

But first, the Celtics had to wait a little while for Russell to join the team. Russell had committed to the US Olympic team, and helped America win the gold medal in Melbourne, Australia. Busy with the Olympics, Russell did not join the Celtics until December 22. When he finally put on his shamrock-green-and-white jersey, he was an immediate force, pulling down 16 rebounds in twenty-one minutes. In his fourth game, he snagged 34 rebounds.

The NBA would be forever changed. Russell could score but was not a scorer in the traditional sense. He played defense. He rebounded. He blocked shots. Russell's defense helped ignite the Celtics' greatest weapon: the fast break.

And he won. With Russell, the Celtics roared to the Finals for the first time, winning a thrilling seven-game series with St. Louis for the first basketball championship in Boston history. In a little over a year, Russell had won a college championship, an Olympic gold medal, and an NBA championship!

The Celtics raced to the Finals again the next year, in a rematch against St. Louis, but Russell injured his ankle in Game 3, and the Hawks took advantage, winning in six games. In the final game of the series, St. Louis beat Boston 110–109, and the Hawks' best player, Bob Pettit, scored 50 points (no three-point shot back then, either). The Celtics were defeated, but they came back hungrier than ever the following season.

What occurred next had never been seen in North American professional sports: the Celtics won the next EIGHT championships in a row!

They were like a machine. Auerbach had drafted

another future Hall of Famer, the great scorer Sam Jones. K. C. Jones—you guessed it, another Hall of Famer—meanwhile, returned from the army in 1958, the year the Celtics won the first of their eight consecutive championships. They would add *another* future Hall of Famer, John Havlicek, in 1962.

Simply put, no one could stop the Celtics.

Not even the arrival of Wilt Chamberlain, the greatest individual force in the history of the game, could stop Boston. Chamberlain joined the Philadelphia Warriors in 1959. He was seven foot one and weighed 275 pounds! He could score at will. He averaged 37.6 points per game in his rookie season and once scored an all-time high 100 points in a game in 1962! To this day, Chamberlain's record for most points scored in a game remains one of the most impressive and unsurpassable feats in sports.

Yet one incredible player does not make a great team. The Celtics played as a team. Wilt scored on Russell the way he scored on the rest, but when it counted, the Celtics had a legion of players who could outdefend, outscore, and outrebound their competitors. In 1962, the Celtics beat the Lakers, who had moved from Minneapolis to Los Angeles, in a classic final against the best scoring duo ever, Jerry West and Elgin Baylor. Baylor even scored 61 points in one game (again, with no three-point shot!), but the Lakers were still no match for the fearsome Celtics. Boston went on to beat Chamberlain again after the Warriors moved to San Francisco. Then they beat Chamberlain another time when he was traded back to Philadelphia after the Syracuse Nationals moved to Pennsylvania and became the 76ers.

In short, the Celtics owned the 1960s.

Auerbach retired after the 1965–66 season, and the Celtics made history of another kind, naming Russell player-coach, a title that's practically unheard of in today's game. Bill Russell became the first African American head coach in the four major team sports.

But even as the Celtics hoisted championship trophy after championship trophy, it was certain that a day would come when the great franchise's streak would end. Finally, in the 1966–67 season, the 76ers were too good. Chamberlain was on a mission. Philly won sixty-eight games that year, demolished the Celtics in five games in the Eastern Conference finals, and the 76ers went on, after so much heartache caused by Boston, to finally win the title.

Yet the Celtics weren't done for good. The next year, the Celtics came back, looking for revenge and eager to reclaim the top spot. In a conference finals rematch with Chamberlain and the defending champion 76ers, Philadelphia went up three games to one. Russell and the Celtics refused to give up, though, and improbably won three straight games, including two on the road, on their way to yet another championship—their ninth in ten years.

As the next season wore on, it became apparent that the Celtics were old and their age was starting to catch up with them. Other teams, like the New York Knicks and Baltimore Bullets (before they eventually became the Washington Wizards), were faster and more athletic. The Celtics came in fourth that regular season yet somehow reached the Finals again. And again, Russell faced Chamberlain, who had been traded to the Lakers.

This time, the Lakers were far better. But the Celtics were the best at doing whatever it took to win championships. They got the job done, winning in seven thrilling games. Russell went out on top, announcing his retirement after the game.

Bill Russell was more than just an NBA legend.

He transformed an entire sport. Basketball was now a major game.

The Celtics' championship victory in 1969 was their ELEVENTH in thirteen years. But the glory of the Celtics ended as the next decade started. After Russell retired, he left behind an irreplaceable void. Boston would return with two championships in three years in the mid-1970s, but wouldn't fully recover as the signature team of the NBA until the arrival of Larry Bird in 1978.

Walter Brown and Red Auerbach's risky long-term commitment to basketball had paid off many times over. Finally, a historic basketball franchise had emerged that deserved to be celebrated alongside other great sports dynasties like the Yankees and Canadiens. Basketball-obsessed kids across the nation shot hoops in parks and driveways, pretending they were on the hardwood court alongside Bill Russell, Bob Cousy, and the other Celtic greats, similar to how kids today throw up half-court shots, filled with dreams of being the next Steph Curry. The Boston Celtics of the '60s were a team that dominated a sport like no other before or since.

THE STORY OF THE 1960s
TOP TEN LIST

For years, the NBA was not the super-glamorous league it is today. Early on, many teams were established in small towns, and sometimes even played games in cities without NBA teams in order to attract new fans, such as when Wilt Chamberlain scored 100 points in a game against the New York Knicks in Hershey, Pennsylvania. The beginnings of the league were very humble. Here is a list of where some NBA teams started and where they now reside.

1. Detroit Pistons: Left Fort Wayne, Indiana, in 1957 to become the Detroit Pistons.
2. Atlanta Hawks: Played home games in Moline, Illinois, as the Tri-Cities Blackhawks before moving to Milwaukee in 1951, then to St. Louis

in 1955, and finally becoming the Atlanta Hawks in 1968.

3. Philadelphia 76ers: Moved from Syracuse, New York, to Philadelphia in 1963 and changed their team name from the Nationals to the 76ers.

4. Washington Wizards: Changed their name from the Chicago Packers to the Zephyrs in 1962, then moved to Baltimore and became the Bullets in 1963, later moved briefly to a suburb of Washington, DC, thirty miles west of the city and changed their name to the Capital Bullets in 1974, then moved back to Washington, DC, proper and changed their name again the following year to the Washington Bullets, and ultimately became the Washington Wizards in 1998.

5. Sacramento Kings: Moved from Rochester, New York, to Cincinnati in 1958 as the Royals, became the Kansas City–Omaha Kings in 1972, then the Kansas City Kings in 1975, and finally moved to Sacramento in 1985.

6. Los Angeles Lakers: Left Minneapolis—the Land of Ten Thousand Lakes—and moved to Los Angeles in 1960 . . . which is funny because

there are hardly any lakes in Los Angeles—it's a desert!

7. Utah Jazz: Left the birthplace of jazz—New Orleans—and moved to Salt Lake City to become the Utah Jazz in 1979. Who goes to Utah to listen to jazz?

8. Golden State Warriors: Moved from Philadelphia to San Francisco in 1962, moved eight miles across the San Francisco Bay to Oakland in 1967, and changed their team name to the Golden State Warriors in 1971.

9. Los Angeles Clippers: Moved from Buffalo, New York, to San Diego and changed their name from the Braves to the Clippers in 1978, and then relocated to Los Angeles in 1984.

10. Oklahoma City Thunder: Moved from Seattle to Oklahoma City and rebranded the team— formerly known as the SuperSonics—as the Thunder in 2008.

THE PLAYERS
OF THE 1960s

ill Russell dominated the decade, leading the Celtics to nine championships in ten years, eventually winning a total of eleven, but the decade was filled with other tremendous players who will never be forgotten. Here are a few:

WILT CHAMBERLAIN

Years: 1959–1973

Position: Center

Height: 7 ft. 1 in.

Teams: Philadelphia–San Francisco Warriors (1959–1964), Philadelphia 76ers (1965–1967), Los Angeles Lakers (1968–1973)

Championships: 2 (1967 76ers, 1972 Lakers)

Most Valuable Player Awards: 4 (1960, 1966, 1967, 1968)

Jersey Number: 13

Nicknames: The Big Dipper, Wilt the Stilt

All-Star Games: 13

Hall of Fame: 1979

Basketball is full of debates. I'd argue Bill Russell was the game's greatest winner and Michael Jordan the game's greatest player. Maybe Oscar Robertson was a better all-around player than Magic Johnson, and maybe Larry Bird was a better shooter than Stephen Curry, but probably not.

However, there is no question as to which player is the greatest single individual force in the history of basketball. That title belongs to one man: Wilton Norman Chamberlain.

When he was attending Overbrook High in Philadelphia, Chamberlain was already six foot eleven. By the time he entered the NBA after playing at the University of Kansas, he had grown to seven foot one and weighed 275 pounds, four inches taller and fifty pounds heavier than Bill Russell.

From the day Chamberlain entered the league, the basketball world changed. He couldn't be moved. His rookie year, Chamberlain averaged 37.6 points and 27 rebounds, leading the league in both categories. Chamberlain led the league in scoring the first seven years he was in the league. He led the league in rebounding eleven times in his fifteen-year career. Russell won the championships, but Chamberlain was so overwhelming the NBA literally changed the rules because of his dominance.

The lane—the rectangle from the foul line to the basket—was widened by four feet because it was too easy for him to score from the low post before the rule was changed. The play of tossing the ball over the backboard so Wilt could catch the pass was outlawed because no one was big or tall enough to challenge him. Being able to touch the ball while it was on the rim had been legal—until Wilt changed what was possible on the court.

His numbers are just comical. Nobody should be able to play that much better than everyone else—but Wilt could. He could score pretty much whenever he wanted. He proved that to be true on the night of March 2, 1962, in Hershey, Pennsylvania, when he scored 100 points against the Knicks.

That's one person scoring *100 points*.

Against Boston in 1960, Wilt grabbed 55 rebounds.

In his third season, Wilt averaged 50.4 points per game.

In his entire career, Michael Jordan scored 50 points 38 times. In 1962 alone, Wilt did it 45 times!

Wilt couldn't do two things: Beat Boston consistently and make foul shots. For all the points Chamberlain scored, he would have scored thousands more had he been able to make a free throw. He tried everything, even shooting underhanded, the old two-handed granny shot. Nothing worked. Wilt missed more than 5,000 foul shots in his career.

Basketball is a team game, but Chamberlain was so big, so dominant, that fans expected him to win every game by himself. When his teams did not win, Chamberlain was blamed for not being as tough in the biggest moments as Russell, for perhaps being selfish or not as hungry, or not having that special something when something special was needed.

In the 1960s, his teams met the Celtics eight times in the playoffs in ten years and lost seven of them. The one time Chamberlain prevailed was in the 1966–67 season with the 76ers. Russell always had better teammates than Chamberlain, but this was the year Philadelphia was the best team in the world, winning sixty-eight games, wiping out the Celtics and ending Boston's streak of eight straight NBA titles.

All of those years, all of those battles, and Wilt only beat Russell in the playoffs one time.

Chamberlain would have to settle for that single victory, for when they met for the final time in the 1969 NBA Finals, Russell won again. By this point, Chamberlain played for the Lakers. Luckily for him, though, the Celtics dynasty couldn't persist forever. Russell retired, and Wilt won another title three years later with another classic team, the fearsome 1971– 72 Lakers, which won a record thirty-three straight games en route to the championship. Chamberlain re- tired following the 1973 season, scoring more points and gathering more rebounds than anyone. No one would ever tower over his peers in the same way again.

OSCAR ROBERTSON
Years: 1960–1974
Position: Point guard
Height: 6 ft. 5 in.
Teams: Cincinnati Royals (1960–1970), Milwaukee
    Bucks (1970–1974)
Championships: 1 (1971 Bucks)

Most Valuable Player Award: 1 (1964)

Jersey Number: 14 (Cincinnati), 1 (Milwaukee)

Nickname: The Big O

All-Star Games: 12

Hall of Fame: 1980

Because the players are so athletic and so much bigger and quicker and faster today than they were in the early days of the NBA, basketball barely has positions. The tallest player usually plays center (though there are exceptions like Dirk Nowitzki), and the shortest usually plays point guard. That's it. Everyone else plays whatever position best suits their skills. Some players commonly play multiple positions. There are even guys who can practically do it all. LeBron James, for example, can play any position on the court.

But in the early 1960s, players mostly played positions according to their height. One player, Oscar Robertson, was different. Robertson was six foot five, 205 pounds, which in those days was the height and weight of a small forward. Robertson, however, was such a good passer, ball handler, and court general that he played point guard. Robertson towered over and overpowered opposing guards, taking advantage of his size when matched up against the likes of Boston's Bob Cousy, who stood at six foot one.

Robertson was the first all-around big guard the game had seen. He could score like a shooting guard but pass like a point guard, rebound like a power forward, and still defend the quicker, smaller players at his position.

He grew up in Indianapolis, Indiana, and went on to be a star player in Cincinnati, when the city still had an NBA franchise. The Royals (known today as the Sacramento Kings) selected him with the first overall pick in the 1960 NBA draft, and he became an immediate high-scoring sensation, averaging 30.5 points as a rookie. In those days, long before the three-point shot, it was an amazing feat to score 30 points in a single game, let alone average such big numbers over the course of a season.

Robertson's outstanding scoring ability was largely a product of his muscular build, which he used to beat up on weaker opponents. Robertson was also a deadeye shooter. He could hit a pull-up jumper off the fast break, but mostly, Robertson would overpower smaller players, backing them down in the post, and shoot over them with his patented turnaround jumper. Robertson would also work a defender to the right baseline and float his shot in from the corner. His many skills made him very difficult to defend.

Today, a big deal is made about scoring a "triple-double"—achieving double figures in three categories, most commonly points, rebounds, and assists, in the same game. In 1961–62, his second year in the league, Robertson *averaged* a triple-double over the seventy-nine games he played: 30.8 points, 12.5 rebounds, and 11.4 assists. In fact, for the first five seasons of his career, he very nearly averaged a triple-double every year, was named to the All-Star team every year from 1961 to 1972, and won the NBA MVP in 1964.

The problem for Robertson, even worse than Wilt Chamberlain, was that his Cincinnati teams were just not good enough to win championships. For all of Robertson's individual achievements, Cincinnati lost to Russell and the Celtics three times in the playoffs, and to Chamberlain and Philadelphia twice. With the Royals, Robertson never reached the Finals, but in 1970, the Royals traded him to Milwaukee, where he teamed with Kareem Abdul-Jabbar and finally, to go along with all of his great passing, scoring and rebounding, won the 1971 NBA title.

ELGIN BAYLOR

Years: 1958–1971

Position: Small forward

Height: 6 ft. 5 in.

Team: Minneapolis–Los Angeles Lakers

Championships: 0

Most Valuable Player Awards: 0

Jersey Number: 22

Nickname: Mr. Inside

All-Star Games: 11

Hall of Fame: 1977

Watch LeBron James sprint downcourt at full speed, leap in the air, and flip the ball into the basket. Watch footage of Kobe Bryant dart into the lane, fade away, and float a jumper into the hoop. Watch the old videos of Michael Jordan soaring, almost looking as though he's trying to decide what magical move to make next *while still in the air . . .*

Now try to imagine basketball without those

moves. Better yet, try imagining basketball with only *one* player with all those moves. That was the state of the NBA during Elgin Baylor's time: slow, plodding, mechanical, and really, compared to today, a little *boring*—until Elgin got the ball and went airborne. Coaches were so strict, they didn't allow players to use fancy dribbles, like a crossover, a move commonly used in today's game where a player bounces the ball from one hand to the other, sometimes putting it through his legs, in an attempt to fake out a defender.

Baylor, a basketball genius from Washington, DC, was the first of the highfliers. While his contemporaries were tossing up one-handed set shots, Baylor was the first player to sweep into the lane, holding the ball in one hand, helping usher basketball into a new age. Baylor wasn't flashy for the sake of showing off, but simply saw the game of basketball differently than the other players of his day. He could leap in the air, which gave him the ability to see over other players. He could hang in the air while driving to the basket, which allowed him to get fouled and still make shots. His combination of speed and quickness and athleticism made him virtually impossible to guard, and once Baylor took flight, everyone else on the court could only stand by and watch.

The Minneapolis Lakers, struggling financially and in serious trouble, drafted Baylor out of Seattle University, and he was immediately a sensation. There were other scoring machines, such as St. Louis power forward Bob Pettit, but Baylor took the game aerial, sweeping and soaring above the rim. Elgin Baylor was the future.

He averaged 24.9 points and 15 rebounds per game his rookie year, but couldn't save the team by himself, as the Lakers were forced to relocate from Minneapolis to Los Angeles in 1959.

Teamed with the great scoring guard Jerry West, the duo was known as Mr. Inside and Mr. Outside. Baylor was Mr. Inside, and even though he was small for a forward by today's standards, he could rebound like a power forward because he was so quick to the ball. He also used his speed to score against bigger opponents, like Bill Russell and Wilt Chamberlain.

How could it be possible that a man who averaged 34.8, 38.3, and 34.0 points per game from 1961–1963, as Baylor did, be considered "underrated"? Part of the reason is that, from a statistical standpoint, Baylor was overshadowed by his peers. Even though Baylor was a remarkable, huge scorer, he never led the league in scoring (which was always hard with a guy like Chamberlain around, who could score 100 points). In fact, Baylor was the most dominant small forward of his time but never led the league in a single major offensive category.

Worse yet, Elgin Baylor owns the title no player ever wants: the greatest player never to win an NBA title. Baylor performed very well in the playoffs, helping the Lakers reach the Finals eight times during his career, including seven against the Boston Celtics between 1959 and 1969. Each time the Lakers matched up against the deadly Celtics, Boston couldn't stop Baylor. In Game 5 of the 1962 Finals in famed Boston Garden, he scored 61 points, which still stands as a Finals record.

But just getting to the championship is never enough. It only *counts* if you leave with the victory. Unfortunately for Baylor, the Lakers squandered their seven chances against the Celtics, losing each time, including three series that ended after an epic seven-game Finals.

But even the great Celtics dynasty couldn't last

forever. In 1970, with the 1960s over and the Celtics dynasty finally dead, the Lakers reached the Finals yet again for an eighth time. But the result was no different. The Lakers lost to the New York Knicks in another seven-game classic.

With bad knees and lots of miles on an aging body, the great Baylor retired nine games into the 1971–72 season—and he quit the game the year the Lakers finally won the NBA championship. Despite the fact that Baylor never won a championship, his individual accomplishments transcended the game. Baylor meant so much to the NBA, not only because he was such a special player, but also because he showed the world that there was more than one way to play basketball. His brand of basketball helped the game evolve into the sport it is today.

JERRY WEST
Years: 1960–1974
Position: Guard
Height: 6 ft. 2 in.
Team: Los Angeles Lakers
Championships: 1 (1972 Lakers)
Most Valuable Player Awards: 0

Jersey Number: 44

Nicknames: Mr. Clutch, Mr. Outside, the Logo

All-Star Games: 14

Hall of Fame: 1980

There are certain names that must be known to understand American history: Washington, Jefferson, Lincoln, Kennedy, and King. In basketball, the same is true, and for the 1960s, Jerry West is one of those names that shaped the history of basketball.

The outline of his body, after all, is the NBA's logo. His nickname was Mr. Clutch. It was as well deserved a nickname as any around. In the 1970 NBA Finals against the Knicks, West hit a 60-foot shot at the buzzer to force the game into overtime. Yes, he almost always lost to the Celtics the same way that Wilt Chamberlain and Elgin Baylor did (they were teammates, of course), but Jerry West was so good that he is also the only player in NBA history to be named MVP of the NBA Finals while playing for the *losing* team. In 1969, West played so brilliantly in the Finals only to see the Celtics win another championship.

Still, despite the Boston shadow looming over him

and the decade, Jerry West was a household name ever since he entered the league, after playing college ball at West Virginia University. Baylor played part of his career in Minneapolis, but West was an original Los Angeles Laker, a signature player of the rise of the NBA on the West Coast.

Like Baylor, West was a fourteen-time All-Star who never won the MVP (again, a feat that was nearly impossible to accomplish with Russell and Chamberlain around), but he and Baylor formed the greatest scoring duo in the history of the NBA. Baylor was Mr. Inside, and West was Mr. Outside because he was known for his excellent perimeter play. As soon as he entered the league, West established himself as a high-scoring guard with the ability to hit shots at will. Baylor would drive to the basket and create while he was in the air. West was a jump shooter. Think about Steph Curry's quick release. At any moment on court, West might just pull up for a jumper. The quick release made him so difficult to guard because if a defender played him too closely, expecting West to shoot, he could dribble right by. The three-point shot was years away, and yet West was deadly. Right when he was about to shoot, he could hesitate and force his man to land into him and draw fouls. In his second year in the league, West averaged 12 free throws per game. He also averaged more than 30 points per game in four different seasons.

Baylor couldn't hold on long enough to win a championship, but West did. West and Chamberlain teamed up in 1971–72 to win sixty-nine games, the most any team had ever won at that point in NBA history. The Lakers that year also won an NBA record thirty-three straight games and rolled to the NBA title, meeting the Knicks and beating them in five games for West's first and only NBA title. After 25,192 points over fourteen years, he had earned it.

Because of the three-point shot, fans today don't mention Jerry West as one of the all-time great shooters, even though he scored more than 25,000 points. But if you're wondering how good Jerry West really was, just think about Jerry West this way: Most point guards in his day averaged 10 to 15 points a game. Jerry West averaged 27 for his career. He was a scoring machine.

There's only one player in the world who can say

that he is *literally* the league's poster boy, his silhouette immortalized in the NBA's logo. Mr. Clutch's story is part of the legend of the NBA, but his impact on the league lives on through the decades.

THE PLAYERS OF THE 1960s
TOP TEN LIST

In the world of professional basketball, the 1960s belonged to Wilt Chamberlain and Bill Russell. Yet, throughout the decade, the NBA was filled with brilliant players who built what would soon become one of the most powerful sports leagues in the world. No knowledge of basketball is complete without knowing just how great these superstars really were. Here is a list of ten players every true student of the game should know:

1. Oscar Robertson (Cincinnati Royals, Milwaukee Bucks): Perhaps the greatest all-around player ever. He once averaged a triple-double throughout an entire season (30.8 points, 12.5 rebounds, 11.4 assists)! He won a championship, a league MVP Award, and

was named to twelve All-Star teams—in short, he did it all.

2. Elgin Baylor (Minneapolis–Los Angeles Lakers): Revolutionized the modern game with his athleticism. He was an original highflier, one of the first to soar through the air and dazzle fans with his leaping ability.

3. Jerry West (Los Angeles Lakers): High-scoring guard who literally became the face of the NBA—his body outline is the NBA logo. He earned the nickname "Mr. Clutch," for his many big-time plays at pivotal moments.

4. Bob Cousy (Boston Celtics): A six-time NBA Champion, Hall of Fame playmaking guard who ran Celtics offense. He was a master of the art of passing, leading the league in assists eight straight years from 1953–1960.

5. Jerry Lucas (Cincinnati Royals, San Francisco Warriors, New York Knicks): Rugged, high-scoring center–power forward who played on weaker teams, but finally nabbed his first—and only—championship victory in 1973. Known for attacking the boards, Lucas averaged over 15 rebounds per game over his career.

6. Hal Greer (Syracuse Nationals/Philadelphia 76ers): A high-scoring guard who was known for his unique foul-shooting technique—he would shoot a jump shot instead of keeping his feet planted. Alongside Chamberlain, he helped the 76ers win the NBA Finals in 1967, snapping the Celtics' eight-year championship streak.

7. Dolph Schayes (Syracuse Nationals/Philadelphia 76ers): A teammate of Greer's whose outside shot was well known for arcing high up in the air.

8. Bob Pettit (Milwaukee–St. Louis Hawks): One of the original high-scoring power forwards of the NBA. He is the only player aside from Kobe Bryant to be named MVP of the NBA All-Star Game four times.

9. Earl Monroe (Baltimore Bullets, New York Knicks): Known as Earl "The Pearl," he was a smooth playmaking guard who could score, too. He teamed up with Walt Frazier to form one of the greatest guard duos in NBA history.

10. Tom Heinsohn (Boston Celtics): Joined Boston the same year as Bill Russell and went on to become a Hall of Famer as both a player and a coach. He won eight championships as a player and two more as a coach.

THE FINALS
OF THE 1960s

~~~~~~

1962: BOSTON CELTICS VS.
LOS ANGELES LAKERS

The Celtics entered the 1961–62 NBA Finals as clear favorites over the Lakers. The Lakers had recently moved from Minneapolis to Los Angeles and posted losing records in their first two seasons in California. But the 1961–62 season proved to be a turning point for the franchise. Elgin Baylor was one of the great young stars of the game, and Jerry West, a high-scoring guard from West Virginia, was drafted by the team in 1960. Early struggles aside, the Los Angeles Lakers were becoming a very good and very dangerous team.

Where the Lakers were still developing, the Celtics

had already come into their own and appeared unstoppable. They had won the championship the previous three years, sweeping the Lakers in four straight games in 1958–59, Baylor's rookie season, and then defeating St. Louis twice to win the 1960 and 1961 titles. Entering the Finals in 1962, the Celtics had won sixty games in the regular season, the most they'd won since Bill Russell joined the team. They were a powerhouse team that was only getting better. The Celtics were so good that in the 1961 Finals, when they beat the Hawks, they had eight future Hall of Fame players, *four of them coming off the bench!*

One of those Hall of Famers, Bill Sharman, retired after the 1961 season, but the Celtics still had seven legends—Bill Russell, Bob Cousy, Tom Heinsohn, Sam Jones, K. C. Jones, Tom "Satch" Sanders, and Frank Ramsey—making up the core of their team. They were bursting with talent.

Still, the 1961–62 playoffs were going to be a big test for the Celtics. They'd won the division by eleven games over the Philadelphia Warriors, but now they had to play the Warriors in the playoffs. Beating Philadelphia meant beating Wilt Chamberlain, who had not only averaged *50.4 points per game* during the season but had also shattered the previous single game scoring record when he poured in 100 points by himself against the Knicks. It was one thing to beat up on the rest of the league and win the division title over Philadelphia during the course of a long season but quite another to have to face them game after game in a short series.

The teams split the first four contests of the playoffs. Russell was not known as a scorer, but after Chamberlain outscored him 42–9 in Game 2, Russell responded with back to back 31-point games.

Game 5 was a brawl—literally. Punches were thrown by both teams. Heinsohn wound up ejected for throwing a punch at Philadelphia's Ted Luckenbill. Chamberlain collided with Sam Jones, which caused Jones to go after Chamberlain, eventually swinging a nearby photographer's chair at Chamberlain! Jones never made contact, but later on, the Celtics' bruising forward Jim Loscutoff threatened the Warriors' Guy Rodgers, who defended himself by picking up that same photographer's chair. It was a wild affair. The Celtics won the heated game, 119–104, and were a win away from the Finals.

Philadelphia, however, had no quit in them. The

Warriors won Game 6, and the two teams engaged in a winner-take-all Game 7: Boston versus Philadelphia, Russell versus Wilt. As one might expect in such a closely fought battle, the game came down to the final shot. Five seconds left, Sam Jones had the ball. Chamberlain rushed out to guard him, but it was too late. Jones nailed the game-winner for a 109–107 win.

The Lakers waited in the Finals. These Lakers were not the same Lakers from two years earlier, a team the Celtics had destroyed. This year, Elgin Baylor had averaged 38.3 points a game, West 30.8. They were the highest-scoring duo in the league and presented a huge challenge for the Celtics.

The Celtics won the first game in Boston, but the Lakers were determined to split their first two match-ups on the road. In Game 2, West and Baylor did what they did best—racked up a ton of points, scoring 40 and 36 respectively, as the Lakers stole the win. In California, the Lakers took the series lead when Baylor (38 points) and West (26) again proved unstoppable, leading to a two-point win.

The game had never seen a combination like West and Baylor. West could shoot from outside, and Baylor, who could drive to the basket and challenge even the great Russell, was a double threat: he could score and also create fouls against the Celtics' big men.

Champions, however, are champions for a reason, and facing a huge three-games-to-one hole if they lost, Boston found a way to win Game 4 in LA, 115–103.

Tied 2-2 in Boston, Baylor put on one of the greatest shows in NBA history, swooping, slashing, and driving his way to an NBA playoff record 61 points in a 126–121 win. He hit 22 shots from the field and was 17-of-19 from the foul line. He'd scored nearly half his team's points. It was a record-setting Finals performance that still stands to this day.

The Lakers were a game away from winning the championship. And they were headed back home to LA. The Celtics, it appeared, had finally met their match.

So what could Boston do?

They did what they'd been doing so well for the last few years: They won. Down 8 at halftime, the Celtics rolled in the second half, outscoring the Lakers by 22 points in the half. The 14-point win set up, yet again, a winner-take-all showdown at Boston Garden.

The Celtics had beaten Chamberlain and Philadelphia. Yet even Chamberlain hadn't put up a performance like Baylor had the last time he'd played in the famed Garden. With the memory of his 61-point night fresh in everyone's mind, Baylor was nearly as good in the deciding game, scoring 41. West was almost as good, netting 35.

Again, the game came down to the final shot. Game tied. The Lakers had the ball. West was covered. Baylor was covered. So Frank Selvy took the shot as time expired. If the shot was true, the Lakers would be champions.

It was up. It was on line.

It missed.

Overtime.

That one missed shot by Selvy, that one defensive stop, gave Boston new life, and they didn't waste it, winning the game—and the title—in OT, 110–107. Some people say the Celtics' good luck saved them. Others say championship teams always find a way. No matter what you believe, the fact of the matter is, Boston emerged as the victor. Four straight titles. To this day, no other NBA team has ever again won four straight. Russell played all fifty-three minutes, scored 30 points, and pulled down *40 rebounds*. The Lakers had come so close, just a basket away from greatness, and obviously left Boston feeling disappointed. Thankfully for Los Angeles fans, their team had a bright future ahead of them with West and Baylor and future stars giving them many more chances to cross the finish line.

1969: BOSTON CELTICS VS. LOS ANGELES LAKERS

The tank was almost empty. The Celtics had won eight of the first nine titles of the decade. Every great player, even the great Wilt Chamberlain, took a backseat to the Celtics' greats. Every celebrated coach of the 1960s, like Alex Hannum in Philadelphia or Red Holzman in New York, was second to Boston's legendary coach Red Auerbach. The Celtics won almost every year. At times, they won easily. Other times, they banded together and won the tough games they maybe should have lost. They also won everything in between.

By 1969, the Celtics' run looked to be over. They were slow. They were old. K. C. Jones had retired in

1967. Cousy, Sharman, and Heinsohn had already retired. Sam Jones, the great sharpshooter, would retire at year's end. Russell hinted that this would be *his* last season, too. Only John Havlicek, the great forward who could run all day, was in his prime.

The Celtics had won those eight straight titles, but Chamberlain and the Philadelphia 76ers had broken the streak in 1967, crushing the Celtics in five games. The Celtics came back in '68, beating Philly and the Lakers to win the title for the tenth time in Bill Russell's twelve-year career. But in 1969, this old Celtics team was looking . . . well, average.

The Lakers, meanwhile, had pulled the equivalent of a superhero team-up in an effort to finally beat Boston, trading for Chamberlain. Now the Lakers had Chamberlain, West, and Baylor, three of the greatest players who ever lived.

The Lakers weren't the only team aiming to take down Boston. A young New York Knicks team was also rising to power, led by dazzling point guard Walt "Clyde" Frazier and center Willis Reed, as was a fast-charging Baltimore Bullets club. In the West, the Milwaukee Bucks had a seven-two rookie named Lew Alcindor, who would later change his name to

Kareem Abdul-Jabbar and who already challenged even Chamberlain with his ability to dominate a game inside.

So it was no surprise when the Celtics finished fourth in the East during the regular season. Going into the playoffs, no one expected much from this Boston squad. How much could you expect from a fourth-place team? It seemed their reign of glory had finally come to an end.

Not so fast.

Boston still had a little gas left in the reserve tank—and the gritty toughness of a champion. The Celtics beat Philadelphia in five games before stunning the Knicks in six. Once more, the championship came down to a face-off between Boston and Los Angeles.

The Lakers had home court advantage. They had Chamberlain. They had West. They had Baylor. They were clearly the better team and were motivated for revenge. All three stars would've won multiple championships if not for Boston, but neither West nor Baylor had ever won a single championship, and Wilt, as great as he was, had only one.

It was like a hammer and a nail, and if you

were a Lakers fan, every year felt like a thump on the head. The Celtics beat them for the title in 1959, 1962, 1963, 1965, 1966, and 1968. They beat Chamberlain in Philly in 1960 and 1962. In 1964, when the Celtics won another title, they had beaten Chamberlain and his San Francisco Warriors, which had moved from Philadelphia in 1963. In 1965, the Warriors traded Chamberlain back to the new team in Philadelphia, the 76ers (the Syracuse Nationals had moved to Philly and changed their name), and Boston promptly beat Philly again in a classic seventh game when Havlicek stole Chamberlain's inbounds pass in the closing seconds. Boston beat Chamberlain in Philly again in 1966 and 1968, losing only in 1967. So everywhere Chamberlain went, whether on the East Coast or the West, Russell and Co. were there to beat him.

The Lakers were furious and focused. Enough was enough. They were the better team. It was time to prove it to the world.

In Game 1 in Los Angeles, both teams refused to accept defeat, and the lead changed hands twenty-one times. West scored 53 points and was ultimately the difference-maker, leading the Lakers to victory. In

Game 2, West and Baylor combined for 72 points on their way to securing a 2-0 series lead.

Boston, full of pride, went home to play Game 3. It was time to change things up or risk going down 0-3 in the series. Bill Russell, acting as player-coach, had opted not to double-team West in the first two games. After losing both matchups, he decided to change his strategy and double-team West on defense. West still scored 24 points, but it wasn't enough to overcome the Celtics, who won the game.

The Celtics finally had some life again. They went into Game 4 determined to even the series. The game proved to be the ugliest matchup of the series, both teams combining for a total of 50 turnovers. With seven seconds left, the Lakers had a one-point lead and prepared to inbound the ball. Baylor received the pass . . . and was ruled out of bounds!

Celtics' ball. It came down to an ugly shot by Jones at the buzzer. The ball somehow sailed out of reach of Chamberlain's hand, bounced on the rim, and fell in to give Boston the win that tied the series at 2-2.

After that sloppy loss, the Lakers returned to their home court and played with fire, winning Game 5. As they headed back to Boston, Los Angeles was one game away from finally winning the championship.

But the Celtics, the team that always found a way to win, did just that and evened the series at three apiece. That set up, once again, a winner-take-all Game 7, this time in Los Angeles.

There they were, the old Celtics, 0-3 on the road in the series but still in the fight. The owner of the Lakers, Jack Kent Cooke, had loaded the ceiling with balloons and called in the University of Southern California marching band, ready for the celebration when the Lakers would finally beat the Celtics, and the balloons would fall. That fired up the old but still proud Celtics.

Throughout the game, the Celtics kept threatening to break it open and go up by an unreachable margin, but the Lakers continued to fight back. A 12-point Boston lead in the first quarter was cut to 3 by the half. In the third quarter, with the Lakers finding themselves in a cold shooting streak, the Celtics extended their lead to fifteen, 91–76.

But there was still a whole quarter left to play. With under six minutes left, the Lakers had narrowed the margin to nine points, 103–96. That was when

Chamberlain came down hard after a rebound. He left the game and wouldn't come back, but the Lakers made a furious final charge, cutting the lead to one with just over a minute remaining.

Maybe the Lakers would get to make good on their celebration plans after all?

Nope. The celebration never came. Instead, the Celtics' Don Nelson hit a desperation shot as the twenty-four-second shot clock was about to expire and Boston's lead was extended to three. The Lakers never closed the gap. Improbably, Boston had won again, 108–106.

Just imagine you're the Lakers, who had come so close once again. It seemed no matter where the great Wilt Chamberlain played, he eventually ran into a Celtics team he couldn't beat. Elgin Baylor? He had now faced the Celtics seven times in the Finals . . . and lost them all. Jerry West had played brilliantly in this series, averaging 37.9 points over the seven games, and was named Most Valuable Player of the Finals. It remains the only time in NBA history the honor has gone to a player on the losing team. Don't you think he would have traded that award for the championship trophy?

When it was over, the Celtics dynasty was complete. Russell retired, and the Celtics were finished after eleven championships in thirteen years, including eight in a row. Russell, Sharman, Cousy, Ramsey, Havlicek, Sam Jones, K. C. Jones, Heinsohn, Sanders, and Auerbach would all be elected into the Hall of Fame. Chamberlain, West, and Baylor may have been better individual players, but no team played as a team and won as a team like the Celtics of the 1960s. It was the stuff of legends, and basketball would never see anything like it again.

THE FINALS OF THE 1960s
TOP TEN LIST

The Boston Celtics dominated the 1960s, winning nine of ten championships, including eight in a row from 1959 to 1966. As unbelievable as that championship run was, here are ten more mind-blowing moments that happened in the 1960s.

1. March 2, 1962: Philadelphia Warriors' Wilt Chamberlain scores a whopping *100* points versus the New York Knickerbockers, setting the single game points record that stands to this day.
2. 1961–62: Chamberlain averaged 50.4 points per game! Another all-time record.
3. 1962 NBA Finals: Los Angeles Lakers' Elgin Baylor scored a record 61 points in Game 5 versus

the Boston Celtics. Despite Baylor's heroic feat, the Lakers would go on to lose the series.

4. 1961–62: Oscar Robertson averaged a triple-double (double-digit averages in three different statistical categories) throughout an entire season (30.8 points, 12.5 rebounds, 11.4 assists). It was the only time a player has ever done so . . . and the "Big O" did it in just his second season in the league!

5. 1961–62: Lakers teammates Jerry West and Elgin Baylor both averaged more than 30 points per game on the season. They averaged over 69 points per game combined.

6. 1962–63: San Francisco Warriors Wilt Chamberlain averaged 44.8 points per game. Somehow, that team lost forty-nine games!

7. 1966: Boston's Bill Russell was named the first African American coach in professional sports. He was still an active player as well, becoming one of only a handful of player-coaches in history.

8. 1966–67: The Philadelphia 76ers won sixty-eight games and the NBA title, ending the Celtics'

record-breaking string of eight straight
championships.

9. 1962 NBA Finals: Bill Russell won Game 7 over
the Lakers with 30 points and . . . 40 rebounds!
His performance wasn't a fluke—he'd also
recorded 40 rebounds in a 1960 Finals game
against the St. Louis Hawks.

10. 1969: The Celtics finished the season in fourth
place—and won the NBA championship yet
again. Their eleventh title in thirteen seasons!

THE
1970s

THE STORY
OF THE 1970s

~~~~~~~~~~~~~~~~~~~~~~~~~~~~~~

CHANGING TIMES

The end of the 1960s and the early '70s changed all major American sports. In football, the AFL and NFL merged in 1970, becoming one league—the NFL—and the Super Bowl era was born. In baseball, the American and National Leagues remained separate, but in 1969, they added extra playoff games. Then, in 1973, the American League added the designated hitter to bat in place of the pitcher, yet pitchers continued to hit in the National League, so each league now had a different set of rules. In 1967, the NHL expanded from its "Original Six" teams, adding six new ones including the Philadelphia Flyers, St. Louis Blues, Los Angeles

Kings, and even a long-lost team called the Oakland Seals.

In basketball, changing times affected the NBA, too, and some of those developments can still be felt today. In fact, in many ways, today's basketball is rooted in these changing times.

Like the other sports, the NBA expanded in the late 1960s. The Chicago Bulls were born. The San Diego Rockets (who soon moved to Houston), Seattle SuperSonics (now the Oklahoma City Thunder) and Portland Trail Blazers soon followed. Unlike baseball and football, however, basketball also saw the rise of a rival league: the American Basketball Association (ABA).

At that point in time, it was hardly clear that America had a need for *one* basketball league, never mind two. The Boston Celtics were the greatest team the league had ever seen, yet the team had difficulty attracting even ten thousand fans per night. (Today's games average twice that amount in person, plus a ton more on TV.) To try to increase fan interest, the NBA used to play doubleheaders in cities that didn't even have a basketball team. For example, the night the Warriors beat the Knicks, and Wilt Chamberlain scored 100 points, the game was played in Hershey, Pennsylvania, miles from Philadelphia or New York.

Even though professional basketball had yet to garner the type of fan bases seen in football or baseball, the rival ABA league was established to compete with the NBA. The NBA's most popular teams were in Boston, Philadelphia, and Los Angeles, so the ABA knew those cities were off-limits. Instead, the ABA formed teams in cities such as Dallas (the Chaparrals) and Pittsburgh (the Pipers), as well as some named after states, such as the Virginia Squires, Utah Stars, and Kentucky Colonels; these latter teams would travel throughout the state to play their home games. The NBA played with the traditional orange ball that remains familiar today. The ABA chose something flashier—a red, white, and blue ball. Both leagues generally played by the same rules, with one major exception: the ABA was the first league to officially adopt a three-point shot.

Yet if the new league was going to be a real rival to the NBA, it needed credibility, and the only way for people to take it seriously was to spend big money and attract great players away from the NBA. Rick Barry, a super-scoring small forward from the

San Francisco Warriors who was known for shooting his free throws underhanded (he led the ABA and NBA in that category a combined five times), jumped to the ABA's Oakland Oaks. Billy Cunningham, who had won a championship with Chamberlain playing for the 76ers, left the NBA for the Carolina Cougars.

The real difference between the two leagues, however, was in style. The ABA played a wide-open, fast-break style of basketball that was less strict fundamentally, yet more athletic and fun to watch. The ABA looked more like the way basketball is played today than the slower, fundamentals-focused NBA.

Every modern basketball fan knows the most exciting play is the slam dunk. Back then, players occasionally dunked in the NBA, but it was usually just the big men like Bill Russell and Chamberlain. In the ABA, smaller players with great leaping ability, such as "Dr. J" Julius Erving, turned the slam dunk into an art form. In the NBA, coaches didn't like players to dribble with fancy moves. In the ABA, players were encouraged to play with more showmanship. They weren't as fancy as the Harlem Globetrotters, those circus geniuses, but ABA players employed the fast playground style seen around courts in large American cities.

Many NBA players and coaches frowned upon the ABA, viewing it as inferior and less professional than the NBA. It was true the NBA had better overall players, but ABA games were becoming more fun not just to play but also to watch. For a sport still struggling to catch on in America, more fun meant more fans.

The differences between the two leagues, and the ways the sport of basketball were evolving, were best exemplified by the ABA's greatest player, "The Doctor" Julius Erving.

No one personified the differences between the two styles of play more than Julius Erving. Elgin Baylor may have been the original superstar who could soar through the air to score, but Erving did everything Baylor could do and more. He was six foot seven, an inch taller than Baylor, with enormous hands that allowed him to palm the basketball as if it were a softball and flip it off his fingertip into the basket, the patented "finger roll." Chamberlain, Russell, and Baylor all used the finger roll, but Erving one-upped them. He would leap from the foul line—fifteen feet from the basket!—elude a defender, and flip the ball into the basket from five or six feet away. Plus, he could take the ball from the baseline and leap in the air to dunk over bigger players.

Michael Jordan famously leaped from the foul line to dunk, causing fans to jump out of their seats, but Erving had done it first; when Jordan did it at the 1988 All-Star Game, he was actually imitating the Doctor, who had first done it at the 1976 ABA All-Star Game. With the arrival of Erving, basketball suddenly looked a whole lot faster, and it was now played in the air, above the rim.

Erving was the most exciting player in America, and he played in the ABA rather the NBA. With his cool style of play and colorful nickname, Dr. J captured the attention of young basketball fans everywhere. Basketball would never look the same. No longer were kids content with just shooting. They wanted to fly, just like the Doctor.

While the ABA was becoming a showplace for talented stars, the NBA was in a period of team-oriented transition. The Celtics dynasty was gone, and for the first few years of the 1970s, the two best teams just happened to play in the country's two largest cities, Los Angeles and New York—the Lakers and Knicks.

Meanwhile, the greatest player was no longer Chamberlain, but Milwaukee's seven-foot-two-inch center Kareem Abdul-Jabbar. Kareem's game was different than Chamberlain's. Rather than using brute force, he dominated the league with the most devastating shot in the history of pro basketball: the skyhook. It was unblockable and equally unstoppable.

The Lakers had finally overtaken the Celtics as the greatest team in the world in 1971–72. They won a record sixty-nine games in the regular season, including a thirty-three-game winning streak, a record that still exists to this day (though Steph Curry and the 2015 Golden State Warriors gave them a run for their money, winning twenty-eight in a row).

In the 1971–72 Finals, the Lakers easily beat the Knicks in a five-game series, finally giving Chamberlain and West a championship as teammates. They would play the Knicks for the title again the following year, the third time in four years the two teams battled for the top spot. The Knicks won the title in '73, and Chamberlain retired, holding virtually every scoring and rebounding record in the book.

West would retire in 1974, along with the great Oscar Robertson, closing the chapter on the many great players of the early 1960s.

John Havlicek was still around, and the Celtics found new life in the mid-1970s. They won two more championships to return to the top of the NBA, but the 1970s were not dominated by one team, or by the same names. The Warriors, frustrated all those earlier years by the Celtics, won the championship in 1975 when Rick Barry returned from the ABA, sweeping the Washington Bullets, a team that would reach the Finals four times in the decade thanks to their two Hall of Fame players, Elvin Hayes and Wes Unseld.

In 1976, after years of competition for fans' attention, the NBA and ABA chose to merge. Despite beginning the season with ten teams, the ABA was constantly struggling financially, and by the end of the playoffs, only six teams remained. Four of those teams—the Indiana Pacers, San Antonio Spurs, Denver Nuggets, and New York Nets—joined the NBA. The other two teams—the Spirits of St. Louis and Kentucky Colonels—folded, and the players who had been stars in the ABA (such as Moses Malone, Artis Gilmore, Dan Issel, George Gervin, George

McGinnis, and Bobby Jones) would instead become great players in the NBA. In order for the Nets to join the league in the same market as the Knicks, they were essentially forced to sell the league's greatest player, the incomparable Dr. J, to the Philadelphia 76ers, where he would team with McGinnis.

The upstart ABA and its red, white, and blue ball was now gone, but its handprints would remain. The NBA was now a more athletic and entertaining league. By 1979, the NBA had even incorporated the ABA's three-point shot, and a new era of professional basketball began that endures to this day.

THE STORY OF THE 1970s

TOP TEN LIST

The American Basketball Association (ABA) and National Basketball Association (NBA) were rivals until the two leagues merged in 1976. Before the merger, the players in the NBA thought it was no contest—of course they were far better than their lesser counterparts in the ABA! Despite their strong belief that the NBA was superior, numerous ABA players who later changed leagues became superstars in the NBA. Here's a list of ten players who proved the talent of the ABA could hold its own on an NBA court.

1. Julius Erving (Virginia Squires, New York Nets, Philadelphia 76ers): The incomparable "Dr. J" was the signature player of the Nets in the ABA

and the 76ers in the NBA. He was one of the originators of the modern dunking style, known for leaping from the foul line to slam the ball in the basket.

2. George Gervin (Virginia Squires, San Antonio Spurs, Chicago Bulls): The smooth point machine of the San Antonio Spurs known as "The Iceman." The Hall of Fame shooting guard led the NBA in scoring four times during his career.

3. Connie Hawkins (Pittsburgh-Minnesota Pipers, Phoenix Suns, Los Angeles Lakers, Atlanta Hawks): Growing up playing pickup basketball on courts around New York City, including the famed Rucker Park, he earned the nickname "The Hawk." He was an impressive force on the Pittsburgh Pipers in the ABA, earning the ABA MVP Award in 1968, and the Phoenix Suns in the NBA. In addition to his time in the ABA and the NBA, Hawkins also played for the masters of trick play, the Harlem Globetrotters.

4. Dan Issel (Kentucky Colonels, Denver Nuggets): High-scoring forward for the entertaining run-and-gun Denver Nuggets teams of the late 1970s

and '80s that were known for taking a ton of shots and scoring a ton of points as a result. The Hall of Famer is a top ten all-time scorer on the combined ABA-NBA list.

5. Artis Gilmore (Kentucky Colonels, Chicago Bulls, San Antonio Spurs, Boston Celtics): Powerful left-handed center who dominated the ABA with Kentucky and the NBA with Chicago and San Antonio. His impact was so immediate that he won both the ABA Rookie of the Year Award and the MVP Award in 1972.

6. Bobby Jones (Denver Nuggets, Philadelphia 76ers): Underrated defensive specialist in the ABA for Denver and in the NBA for Philadelphia. A productive player who routinely came off the bench, Bobby Jones won the first-ever NBA Sixth Man Award.

7. Moses Malone (Utah Stars, Spirits of St. Louis, Buffalo Braves, Houston Rockets, Philadelphia 76ers, Washington Bullets, Atlanta Hawks, Milwaukee Bucks, San Antonio Spurs): Relentless rebounder and scorer who helped take Houston to the NBA Finals in 1981, and then went on to win the title with Philadelphia in 1983, earning

the Finals MVP Award. The three-time NBA MVP is considered one of the greatest centers ever to play the game.

8. David Thompson (Denver Nuggets, Seattle SuperSonics): Legendary slam-dunk king who earned the moniker "The Skywalker." He once scored 73 points in an NBA game, one of only five players ever to top 70 points. He was drafted first overall in both the 1975 ABA and NBA Drafts, and chose to initially play for Denver in the ABA.

9. Spencer Haywood (Denver Rockets, Seattle SuperSonics, New York Knicks, New Orleans Jazz, Los Angeles Lakers, Washington Bullets): Dominant Hall of Fame scoring center who earned both the ABA Rookie of the Year Award and the MVP Award in his first season after averaging 30 points and just under 20 rebounds per game.

10. George McGinnis (Indiana Pacers, Philadelphia 76ers, Denver Nuggets): Great scoring big man and All-Star for the Indiana Pacers in both the NBA and ABA. Went to 1977 NBA Finals with Philadelphia, and won two ABA championships.

THE PLAYERS
OF THE 1970s

~~~~~~~~~~~~~~~~~~~~~~~~~~~~~~~~~~~~~

There were so many great players in the 1970s as the game blossomed into an acrobatic, athletic art form, especially across two leagues. In the ABA, there were George Gervin and David Thompson (who would both be stars in the NBA into the 1980s) and Nate "Tiny" Archibald (who is still the only player in NBA history to lead the league in points AND assists in the same season), Elvin Hayes, and Wes Unseld, Pete Maravich, Connie Hawkins, Walt Frazier, Willis Reed, Gail Goodrich, and Earl Monroe. But the following five players truly stood above the rest.

KAREEM ABDUL-JABBAR
Years: 1969–1989

Position: Center

Height: 7 ft. 2 in.

Teams: Milwaukee Bucks (1969–1975), Los Angeles Lakers (1976–1989)

Championships: 6 (1971 Bucks; 1980, 1982, 1985, 1987, 1988 Lakers)

Most Valuable Player Awards: 6 (1971, 1972, 1974, 1976, 1977, 1980)

Jersey Number: 33

Nickname: Cap

All-Star Games: 19

Hall of Fame: 1995

Wilt Chamberlain was the most dominant physical force the game has ever seen, but no one has ever perfected the ultimate scoring weapon like Kareem Abdul-Jabbar. His skyhook is still the most original, unstoppable shot in the history of basketball.

That's why Abdul-Jabbar is the NBA's all-time leading scorer. Bill Russell retired the year before he entered the league, so the two legends never met on the court, but when he went against Chamberlain, the two battled fiercely, the young superstar with a big future against the aging legend who had set the standard for dominance.

Kareem was born Ferdinand Lewis Alcindor Jr. in New York City and was a dominant player from the very start. He was six foot eight inches tall at Power Memorial Academy high school, and his teams were overpowering. Though UCLA won its first championship in 1964, it was Lew Alcindor who truly began the UCLA dynasty during his college career.

Alcindor was statistically dominant like Chamberlain and was a winner like Russell. He won three championships in high school and three more at UCLA. He was drafted first overall by Milwaukee in 1969 and won the NBA Rookie of the Year Award in a landslide, having averaged 28.8 points and 14.5 rebounds per game. In his second year, Milwaukee won its first-ever NBA championship in a four-game sweep over the Baltimore Bullets (now the Washington Wizards), and Kareem was the playoff MVP.

While at UCLA, Alcindor converted from Catholicism to Islam, but he did not change his name to Kareem Abdul-Jabbar until 1971. Jabbar idolized Jackie Robinson and was a very political athlete, routinely speaking out against racism and injustice.

His outspokenness did not always make him a popular player with the public, but he, along with Bill Russell, Robinson and Hank Aaron in the MLB, and Jim Brown in the NFL, was one of the most vocal advocates in sports during the civil rights movement.

Kareem was the master of the skyhook, which made him the most dangerous force in the game because the shot was virtually impossible to defend. Kareem would extend his arm in an arc formation and release the ball so that it was out of reach of his defender.

Kareem won the league MVP three times in his first five seasons (and would win a record six times overall). He led the league in scoring twice and averaged over 30 points a game in four different seasons. He led the league in blocked shots four times and rebounds once. Kareem could do it all and played both sides of the court like a master.

Being seven foot two helped make Kareem's skyhook so unstoppable because he towered over most defenders, but a lot of guys in the NBA who were also seven feet or over couldn't master Kareem's signature shot. Abdul-Jabbar was a master of footwork, head fakes, and ball fakes, which allowed him to create enough space to get his shot away untouched. All Kareem needed were a couple of inches of room, and once he rose up to shoot, it was estimated that his arm was nearly eleven feet from the ground, essentially looking down on the basket when he shot. No wonder no one could ever block him.

Three years after winning the title, the Bucks reached the NBA Finals again in 1974, where they lost a seven-game classic against the Celtics. Kareem was the best player in the game, but he had a problem: Isolated and unhappy, he did not want to play in Milwaukee and was traded to the Los Angeles Lakers in 1975. For a time, after Wilt Chamberlain retired in 1973, the Lakers were weak, but the drafting of Earvin "Magic" Johnson and the acquisition of Kareem resurrected the Lakers into the 1980s. Kareem won five more championships in 1980, 1982, 1985, 1987, and 1988.

For nineteen years, Kareem was the difference-maker in the NBA, following the path of big-man dominance laid by Russell and Chamberlain. When he retired after the 1989 season, he had done the unthinkable: he had passed Chamberlain as the all-time leading scorer in NBA history, with 38,387 total points, and was arguably its greatest player as well.

JULIUS ERVING

Years: 1971–1987

Position: Small forward

Height: 6 ft. 7 in.

Teams: Virginia Squires (ABA, 1971–1973), New York Nets (ABA, 1973–1976), Philadelphia 76ers (1976–1987)

Championships: 3 (1974, 1976 Nets ABA; 1983 76ers)

Most Valuable Player Awards: 4 (1974, 1975, 1976 ABA; 1981)

Jersey Number: 32 (Virginia, New York), 6 (Philadelphia)

Nicknames: Dr. J, the Doctor

All-Star Games: 16 (5 ABA, 11 NBA)

Hall of Fame: 1993

No player exemplified the possibilities of basketball like the Doctor. Any moves kids dreamed of seeing on the hard court, the incomparable Dr. J could make a reality. In the 1960s, Elgin Baylor opened the door to basketball being a more athletic game, but in the '70s, Dr. J transformed basketball into the creative game it is now.

There was nothing Julius Erving couldn't do. He was born on February 22, 1950, in Hempstead, Long Island, New York, and was gifted with a sense of athletic grace. He had huge hands, so the Doctor could palm the basketball, jump from the foul line, and dunk. He could run the baseline, jump in the air on the right side of the basket, and flip the ball into the basket from the left side. No one had ever seen a player hang in the air like that.

Dr. J wrote new basketball rules. The old coaches said players weren't supposed to leave their feet to pass. Erving would leap in the air and stay up there while he decided what to do. Some older coaches thought he was too fancy, a show-off, but kids loved watching him play and spent hours on the basket-ball court trying to copy just one of the unbelievable moves he made famous.

Upon joining the NBA with Philadelphia in 1976, Dr. J transformed a team that had won just nine games—yes, *nine* games!—in the 1972–73 season into one of the best teams in the Eastern Conference. Erving led the 76ers to the Finals in 1977, where they ultimately lost to the Portland Trail Blazers. The 1977 NBA Finals were known for three things: Erving's fast-break dunk on Bill Walton, the hulking Trail Blazers center, and the 76ers winning the first two games, then losing four straight and the title.

Fortunately for Erving, it wouldn't be his last shot at the crown. Another all-time great, Moses Malone, joined the 76ers before the start of the 1982–83 season. Malone and Erving proved to be a formidable duo and won the NBA championship that same year.

Erving was known for his thunderous dunks, grace, and amazing creativity. Even more than Kareem Abdul-Jabbar, it was the great Dr. J who was the most popular player in basketball during the 1970s. There would be other great leapers and dunkers after, but there would only be one Dr. J.

BILL WALTON
Years: 1974–1987
Position: Center

Height: 6 ft. 11 in.

Teams: Portland Trail Blazers (1974–1978), San Diego–Los Angeles Clippers (1979–1985), Boston Celtics (1985–1987)

Championships: 2 (1977 Trail Blazers, 1986 Celtics)

Most Valuable Player Awards: 1 (1978)

Jersey Number: 32 (Portland, San Diego), 5 (Boston)

Nickname: The Big Redhead

All-Star Games: 2

Hall of Fame: 1993

Basketball is a big man's game. Ever since the career of George Mikan, the leader of the Minneapolis Lakers of the late 1940s and '50s, the NBA's first dynasty, then on to Bill Russell, Wilt Chamberlain, and Kareem Abdul-Jabbar, the game has often been dominated by the big man in the middle.

Bill Walton was the next in that great line of centers. He had wild red hair that he kept under control by wearing a headband. He wore a big red beard, too. He told everyone he was six foot eleven, but everyone knew he was really seven foot one or even as tall as seven two, but he thought people treated seven-footers differently and didn't want to be called one. The truth about his height was a question, but there was no debate about his greatness. In college, Walton had a ridiculously successful career at UCLA, where he followed Abdul-Jabbar and kept the Bruins dynasty alive with one of the greatest games in college history. In the 1973 NCAA Men's Basketball Finals, Walton hit 21 of 22 shots in the win over Memphis State, scoring 44 of UCLA's 87 points.

Walton was taken with the first overall pick in the draft by the Portland Trail Blazers and was an instant star. Centers were always known to score and rebound, but Walton was different. Not only could he do both, but he was also quite possibly the best passer anyone had ever seen at that height.

There was only one problem with Walton, and it was a really, really big problem: Bill Walton could never stay healthy. When he was on court, he was one of the greatest players who ever lived. He understood basketball—where to position himself to get rebounds, how to time his jumps in the air, when to make that perfect pass to a teammate cutting to the hoop—but no other player in NBA history missed more games due to injury than Bill Walton. Walton represented the other side of the game, the price the body pays for running, jumping, cutting, stepping on players awkwardly, and getting awkwardly stepped on. His body couldn't take the punishment.

How, then, did Bill Walton become a signature player of the game when he was hurt all the time? Because people remembered how dominant Walton had been at UCLA, and because he was fantastic in 1976–77 when he was mostly healthy. He still missed seventeen games due to injury, but when he came back, he led a young group of Trail Blazers all the way to the NBA Finals, where they met a great Philadelphia team led by ABA stars "Dr. J" Julius Erving and George McGinnis. The 76ers looked too athletic, too good, too fast, winning the first two games of the series. Yet Walton and his team were great and steady, and won the next four games, stunning the talented 76ers in six games. Walton was named the Finals MVP.

He would go on to win the league MVP Award the following season, helping the Trail Blazers win fifty of their first sixty games before he fell once more to injury. Walton returned to action in the playoffs, only to be sidelined by injury yet again, forcing him to sit on the bench after the second game of the series. Without his skill and leadership, Portland lost the series to Seattle.

Walton was never as good again, although he made a successful comeback with the Celtics for one year in 1985–86, winning another championship. Injuries greatly limited Walton's career, and the basketball world was left wondering just how good he might have become had he ever been healthy enough to reach his true potential.

JOHN HAVLICEK

Years: 1962–1978

Position: Guard-forward

Height: 6 ft. 5 in.

Team: Boston Celtics

Championships: 8 (1963, 1964, 1965, 1966, 1968, 1969, 1974, 1976)

Most Valuable Player Awards: 0

Jersey Number: 17

Nickname: Hondo

All-Star Games: 13

Hall of Fame: 1984

If you can imagine having an endless supply of oxygen in your lungs, you could feel what it was like to be John Havlicek, the greatest link of the 1960s Celtics to the two championships Boston won in the 1970s. Havlicek could run all day. It seemed to his opponents that he never, ever got tired.

When the Celtics were the kings of the NBA in the 1960s, Havlicek came off the bench as one of the first true "sixth men," and won four straight championships to start his career after being drafted out of Ohio State. Then he won two more in 1968 and 1969 to close out the decade. After Russell retired in 1969, the Celtics weren't the same team they'd been throughout the earlier years of the decade. But a few years later, the Celtics returned to power, and in the 1972–73 season, they won sixty-eight games and appeared on a collision course with the Lakers once more in the Finals.

It was not to be. Havlicek injured his shoulder in the playoffs, and in the Eastern Conference finals, Boston lost to the Knicks in a seventh game at Boston Garden.

Havlicek was already popular by the 1970s. It was Havlicek who famously stole Wilt Chamberlain's inbound pass in the final seconds of the 1965 Eastern Conference finals against Philadelphia; Havlicek who ran up and down the court, never tired, knocking in bank shots and runners and leaners. It was Havlicek who scored 40 points when the Celtics won their tenth championship, in 1968, over the Lakers. He was one of the great mid-range scorers, able to take the ball to the basket or pull up for his reliable jump shot.

Havlicek was at his very best in the 1974 Finals against Kareem Abdul-Jabbar and the Milwaukee Bucks. The Celtics had not won a championship since Russell retired, and the year earlier, Havlicek's injury was the biggest reason they had lost to the Knicks. He made up for it in 1974, putting on a spectacular performance in an Eastern Conference Final rematch against the Knicks, averaging 29.4 points as the Celtics won in five games.

Against the Bucks, who in addition to Abdul-Jabbar also had a young star named Bobby Dandridge as well as the aging but great Oscar Robertson, Havlicek was terrific in a classic sixth game at Boston Garden, the Celtics with a chance to win the title at home. In a two-overtime thriller, Havlicek matched Abdul-Jabbar shot for shot, and he eventually outscored Kareem 36–34. Havlicek swished a floater over Kareem for a 101–100 lead and what seemed like the championship-winning bucket, but Kareem nailed an 18-foot skyhook to force a seventh game in Milwaukee. The Celtics won the championship anyway, beating the Bucks on their home court, 102–87, for championship number twelve, and Havlicek's seventh.

When Russell retired, it was Havlicek in the 1970s who kept the connection to the glory days, and two years after the Celtics' victory over the Bucks, they won the championship again in 1976. Havlicek retired in 1978 as Boston's all-time leading scorer. He never won a league MVP, never won a scoring title, but all John Havlicek did was everything a team needed to raise a championship banner at the end of the year. He was as great a winner as any player who ever graced the court.

RICK BARRY
Years: 1965–1980
Position: Small forward
Height: 6 ft. 7 in.
Teams: San Francisco Warriors (1965–1967), Oakland Oaks (ABA, 1968), Washington

Capitols (ABA, 1969), New York Nets (ABA, 1970–1972), Golden State Warriors (1972–1978), Houston Rockets (1978–1980)

Championships: 2 (1969 Oaks ABA; 1975 Warriors)

Most Valuable Player Awards: 0

Jersey Number: 24 (San Francisco, Oakland, Washington, New York, Golden State), 2 and 4 (Houston)

Nickname: The Miami Greyhound

All-Star Games: 12 (8 NBA, 4 ABA)

Hall of Fame: 1987

Like Jerry West and John Havlicek, Rick Barry was a scoring machine from the day he entered the NBA out of the University of Miami in 1965. Barry was drafted by the San Francisco Warriors and in his second season won the scoring title with an average of 35.6 points per game. With Barry in the mix, the Warriors were immediate contenders, beating the two dominant teams of the Western Conference in the 1967 playoffs. They swept Jerry West and the Lakers in the first round and beat the St. Louis Hawks (now the Atlanta Hawks) to reach the NBA Finals.

The only problem for Barry in his first NBA Finals

was his upstart Warriors were pitted against one of the greatest teams in the history of the NBA: the sixty-eight-win 1967 Philadelphia 76ers led by Wilt Chamberlain. Philadelphia, having lost to Boston for so many years, was not to be denied. Barry averaged 40.8 points per game for the series, but Chamberlain averaged 28.5 rebounds to go with 18 points and the Sixers won in six games.

As great as he was on the court, Rick Barry was not always well liked as a player, but he was an individual who wasn't afraid to stand up for himself. He even shot his free throws "granny style" (underhanded), led the league seven times in free-throw percentage, and would retire with the highest percentage ever (.900). When the rival ABA was formed, Barry was one of the first star players to make the leap. Unhappy with his salary, Barry agreed to move across the Bay to play for the newly formed Oakland Oaks. The NBA wasn't about to let him get away that easily, though. The league sued Barry and prevented him from playing in 1967. Eventually, he was permitted to join Oakland in the 1968–69 season, and he did not disappoint. Barry scored 34 points a game, and the Oaks won the ABA title.

Like many ABA teams, the Oaks struggled to draw fans and were forced to move to Washington, DC. Frustrated with the situation, Barry was moved to the New York Nets, where he played for two years, but the legal issues surrounding his contract were not over. In 1972, the court forced him to return to the Warriors, and once again, they were instant contenders, a young team that now had a legendary scorer and passer.

In 1975, the Warriors, with Barry leading the charge, rolled over Washington in the Finals in a four-game sweep for their first NBA title. Barry, devastating from the outside, was named Most Valuable Player of the Finals.

Over the next couple of years, bad knees began to eat at Barry's effectiveness. He would never play for a championship again, but for the first ten years of his career, a Rick Barry team was always a very, very dangerous one. He was simply an expert at getting the ball in the basket, and his record speaks for itself: he is the only player in history who led the league in scoring at least once each in the NCAA, ABA, and NBA.

THE PLAYERS OF THE 1970s
TOP TEN LIST

The ABA lasted nine years, and while some of its greatest players like Dr. J, Moses Malone, and George Gervin went on to flourish in the NBA, some of the ABA greats played their best years with the red, white, and blue ball. Here are ten players who shone when the ABA was at its height.

1. Roger Brown (Indiana Pacers, Memphis Sounds, Utah Stars): Hall of Fame, high-scoring forward during the Indiana Pacers' glory years, in which they won three ABA championships.

2. Mel Daniels (Minnesota Muskies, Indiana Pacers, Memphis Sounds, New York Nets): Fourth-leading ABA scorer in history and another Hall

of Fame member of the Pacers during their championship run.

3. Larry Brown (New Orleans Buccaneers, Oakland Oaks/Washington Caps/Virginia Squires, Denver Rockets): Before he was a great coach at both the professional and collegiate levels, he was a star point guard in the ABA.

4. Louie Dampier (Kentucky Colonels, San Antonio Spurs): All-time leading ABA scorer and a top point guard in the league who was one of very few players to play in all nine seasons of the ABA's existence.

5. Mack Calvin (Los Angeles Stars, The Floridians, Carolina Cougars, Denver Nuggets, Virginia Squires, Los Angeles Lakers, San Antonio Spurs, Utah Jazz, Cleveland Cavaliers): Standing at only six feet tall, the well-traveled, high-scoring guard couldn't be stopped. He was named to five ABA All-Star teams.

6. Ralph Simpson (Denver Rockets/Nuggets, Detroit Pistons, Philadelphia 76ers, New Jersey Nets): The lanky, six-foot-five-inch shooting guard was a five-time ABA All-Star and the

highest all-time scorer for Denver while they were in the ABA.

7. Trooper Washington (Pittsburgh-Minnesota Pipers, Los Angeles Stars, The Floridians, New York Nets): Standing at six foot seven, he played center against taller guys, holding his own, and led the league in field goal percentage twice.

8. Steve Jones (Oakland Oaks, New Orleans Buccaneers, Memphis Pros, Dallas Chaparrals, Carolina Cougars, Denver Rockets, Spirits of St. Louis, Portland Trail Blazers): "The Snapper" played all nine years that the ABA was around, earning three trips to the ABA All-Star Game. Today, he's a commentator for NBA TV games.

9. Warren Jabali (Oakland Oaks, Washington Caps, Indiana Pacers, The Floridians, Denver Rockets, San Diego Conquistadors): Rugged guard who could nail the three-pointer. He won the Rookie of the Year Award in 1969 and was also a four-time All-Star.

10. Doug Moe (New Orleans Buccaneers, Oakland Oaks, Carolina Cougars, Virginia Squires): Led the league in points in his rookie season. The

three-time ABA All-Star small forward won the ABA Championship in 1969 with the Oakland Oaks. Following his playing days, he went on to become a successful NBA coach, winning the NBA Coach of the Year Award in 1988.

THE FINALS
OF THE 1970s

~~~~~~

1970: NEW YORK KNICKS
VS. LOS ANGELES LAKERS

For decades, New York has been called the basketball capital of the world. It earned that title because of the great college basketball games of the 1940s and 1950s played in the storied arena Madison Square Garden, and the world's most famous touring basketball team, the Harlem Globetrotters. It earned that title because of the early greats, like Dolph Schayes, Bob Cousy, Julius Erving, and Kareem Abdul-Jabbar, who came from the city and the area, as well as coaches like Red Auerbach and Al McGuire. It earned that title because as basketball became more of a predominantly African American game, a city game, the famous Rucker League in Harlem was the place where the best players, from Wilt Chamberlain to Connie Hawkins, Tiny Archibald to Julius Erving, came to show off their stuff. If you were a great player, you came to Rucker Park, the greatest playground proving ground in America.

New York did not, however, earn the title of the capital of the basketball world because of its professional team, the Knickerbockers. The Knicks were awful for many years. While Minneapolis, Boston, Philadelphia, Los Angeles, and St. Louis were the cities playing for the NBA title in the early days of the NBA, New York was an also-ran. They did appear in three straight Finals, in 1951, 1952, and 1953, yet lost each. During the great Celtics run of the '60s the Knicks did not even make the playoffs for several years.

That finally changed in the late 1960s, when the Knicks put together a slick, fast powerhouse squad. As the Celtics faded away after the 1969 Finals, the Knicks took over. They'd been on the cusp when the Celtics had stunned them in the 1969 playoffs, but in 1970, the Knicks matured and met the Lakers in the Finals.

So much was riding on this. The Knicks were the young upstarts, but no one denied their toughness and talent. Four players on that Knicks team—point guard Walt "Clyde" Frazier, forward Dave DeBusschere, small forward Bill Bradley, and center Willis Reed—and their head coach, Red Holzman, who was a native New Yorker, would wind up in the Hall of Fame.

The Knicks were great in 1970. They won sixty games and ran through another young upstart team—Baltimore—in the first round and another in the Milwaukee Bucks, who were led by rookie Lew Alcindor (in the days before he changed his name to Kareem Abdul-Jabbar).

The Lakers, their hearts having been broken all those years by the Celtics, didn't have to worry about Boston anymore. Russell and the Celtics dynasty were gone, but Chamberlain and Jerry West—the core of the Lakers—were still playing. Seven times the Lakers had been in the Finals. Seven times they had lost to Boston. Going into the Finals against the Knicks, the Lakers were the older, more seasoned team. The Knicks had won fourteen more games than the Lakers in the regular season, but Los Angeles' years of play-off experience gave them the edge against a New York team entering the Finals for the first time.

The first two games took place in New York. In Game 1, the Knicks started strong and amassed an early double-digit lead and never relented. The Knicks' big center Willis Reed outplayed Chamberlain, and the Knicks won in a rout, 124–112.

In Game 2, the Lakers turned the tables and jumped out to an early double-digit lead, but they weren't able to maintain it throughout the game like the Knicks had in the first matchup. With the clock winding down and the game tied, Jerry West hit two free throws, bringing his points total to 34 for the game, and gave his team the two-point lead they needed for the win.

The teams went to Los Angeles for Game 3, and it turned out to be an unforgettable matchup. The two teams battled each other all game, playing physical basketball so intense that Elgin Baylor ended up fouling out. Under a minute left in the game and the Knicks were up by two. LA's ball. Who else would you want taking the potential game-tying shot but the great Jerry West? It was a no-brainer. West launched a 20-footer that went in with fifteen seconds remaining. It looked like overtime was in the cards.

Dave DeBusschere had other ideas. With three seconds left, DeBusschere nailed a 15-footer from the foul line to give New York a 102–100 lead.

The Lakers had one last chance.

Chamberlain inbounded the ball and gave it to West, who threw it sixty-three feet in desperation with no time left—and it went in! Today, West's shot would have been a three-pointer, and the Lakers would have won the game. In 1970, there was no three-point shot in the NBA, and that made all the difference. West's long-distance shot only got the Lakers to overtime, where they ended up losing anyway, 111–108.

Game 4 also went to overtime! The Lakers desperately needed to come out on top in this one to even the series. They did, 121–115, behind 30 points from Baylor and 37 from West.

The series went back to New York, and after taking an early lead in Game 5, the Knicks struggled in the third quarter after their leader, Reed, injured his hip. The Knicks fought back, determined to win it for their captain, and overcame a double-digit third quarter lead and took Game 5, putting them just a game away from the title. But the win was bittersweet—Reed, who had been fantastic all season and had outplayed Chamberlain throughout the first few games, was now sidelined. So close to their first-ever championship, New York was forced to play without their best player.

When the series went back to Los Angeles for Game 6, the Knicks showed how much not having Reed hurt them all. Chamberlain scored 45 points, and the Lakers demolished New York, 135–113, sending the series back to fabled Madison Square Garden for a winner-take-all seventh game.

The Lakers were more than ready. They remembered all those years against Boston without winning a seventh game and felt like this was finally their year. The Knicks were trying to be optimistic, yet everyone had the same thought: How could they win without Reed?

Just before tipoff, a roar swept over the 19,500 in attendance. Hobbling down the runway to the court was Reed! He could barely walk, but there he was in uniform.

The place went wild! Reed was going to play. Clearly in pain, he limped to the center for a jump ball against the mighty Chamberlain. He nailed his first shot. And then his second. The Lakers looked demoralized.

Those were the only two baskets Reed would score throughout the game, but they were enough to make the Knicks suddenly believe they could win. Reed may have stalled offensively, but he played solid defense against Chamberlain, and his teammates made up for it on the offensive end. Frazier scored 36. Dick Barnett scored 21. Final score: Knicks 113, Lakers 99.

The Knicks had won their first championship, bolstered not by talent but by the heart of their leader. It was the greatest moment in Knicks' history . . . and one of the most inspirational moments in sports, period.

The Lakers' moment would come, but for yet another season, they had fallen just short.

1976: Boston Celtics vs. Phoenix Suns

Game 5. Game 5? Game 5! To this day, forty years later, it is still called the wildest, craziest, greatest Finals game in NBA history. It is *the* game by which all Finals games are judged. Maybe the 1984 Game 4 Celtics-Lakers slugfest matches it, or maybe 1998 Game 6 Bulls-Jazz or the 2013 Finals Game 6 Spurs-Heat comes close, but no game yet in NBA history tops what happened June 4, 1976, at the Boston Garden.

Two years earlier, the Celtics had reemerged as the league leader, winning their twelfth championship. The Celtics had three future Hall of Famers on that team—John Havlicek, the burly left-handed center Dave Cowens, and the sharpshooting guard Jo Jo White. A fourth, Don Nelson, another holdover from the Russell years, would be inducted into the Hall as a head coach. A fifth, their current coach Tommy Heinsohn, was already in the Hall of Fame as a player. The Celtics were, well, again the Celtics.

As a franchise, the Suns weren't even ten years old. They were founded when the NBA expanded in 1968, and Phoenix wasn't even a good team, really. They'd gone 42-40 in the regular season, finishing third in the Western Conference, and had a few skilled players, like the rookies Alvan Adams and Ricky Sobers. Yet in history and talent, they appeared vastly overmatched compared to the Celtics.

But the Suns got hot when it mattered—in the playoffs. They even upset Rick Barry and the defending champion Warriors in seven games in the Western Conference finals. They were playing as a team and with confidence. They also had former Celtic Paul Westphal, who had been on the 1974 championship team. Now here they were, strangely enough, playing the legendary Celtics for a title.

The Celtics cruised through the first two games in Boston, and it looked like the Celtics might be heading for an easy four-game sweep. Then things got nasty. Phoenix didn't like how rough and rugged the Celtics were. They thought Boston's muscle—Cowens—and power forward Paul Silas played dirty.

In Game 3 in Phoenix, Sobers and Celtics forward Kevin Stacom had ended up in a fistfight under the basket. Both players were ejected. The Suns got mad and went on a scoring spree to take a 23-point lead in the third quarter, but the Celtics knew better than to give up. Boston came back and was down by just 2 points near the end of the fourth quarter. Phoenix rallied from there, though, and won the game, showing Boston they weren't a bunch of pushovers.

Game 4 was another close game—and another physical contest, to put it mildly. The two teams were whistled for 21 fouls in the first ten minutes of the game! That's more than 2 fouls per minute! Ultimately, the Suns just barely outplayed the Celtics, 109–107, tying the series at 2-2.

In Boston for Game 5, Boston was ready to put the Suns back in their place. They led 42–20 at one point in the first half. Yet the Suns kept fighting and had pulled to within 9 in the fourth quarter. They were relentless, mounting a comeback Boston fans were not used to seeing from opposing teams, especially in the famed Boston Garden, where teams usually cracked under the pressure. Phoenix even took the lead 95–94 with twenty-two seconds left, but then the Celtics tied it up. Phoenix had one last chance to win in regulation but never got a shot off.

Overtime.

The Celtics opened up a 4-point lead in overtime, but Phoenix again clawed back. The Suns' power forward Garfield Heard nailed a jumper to tie it at 101 with forty-five seconds left. Once again, Phoenix had a chance to win it on the final shot, but Sobers lost the ball, giving the Celtics a chance to win it. Havlicek took the ball in the corner, poised to sink the game-winner . . . and missed.

Double overtime!

By now, Alvan Adams, the Suns' rookie center, had fouled out. Celtics' shooting guard Charlie Scott had also fouled out. Boston's Jo Jo White was still around, though, and he just kept firing, raining in jumpers from all over the court. But after a Sobers basket and foul shot, the Suns held a 106–105 lead. Remarkably, over the course of fifty-six minutes of basketball, through a complete regulation game and one overtime period, this was only Phoenix's second lead of the day.

They wouldn't hold it for long. The Celtics came right back with a bucket, and then Cowens seemed to ice the game with a jumper . . . but no! He was called for an offensive foul, fouling out. The crowd buzzed with excitement and rage as Cowens left the court.

Boston held defensively, and then a runner by Jo Jo White gave them a 109–106 lead with nineteen seconds left. Garfield Heard inbounded the ball to Dick Van Arsdale, who nailed a quick jumper, pulling the Suns to one point, 109–108.

Boston's Jim Ard tried to inbound the ball to Havlicek, but Westphal, the former Celtic, raced in, stole the pass, tossed the ball to Van Arsdale, who passed to power forward Curtis Perry . . . who missed the shot! Perry grabbed his own rebound, though, and nailed the second attempt, a jumper.

How could this be? Down by three with 19 seconds left and now up 110–109 with five seconds left! The crowd was stunned. The Celtics were stunned.

This wasn't happening. The barely-above-.500 Suns were five seconds away from beating Boston and going home to Game 6 with a chance to beat the mighty Celtics and win their first NBA championship.

After a timeout, Nelson inbounded to Havlicek at mid-court. With most people expecting the Celtics to try to get the ball to White, Havlicek kept the ball instead. He drove past three Suns guarding the paint, leaned toward the basket, and actually began falling down as he got a shot off with time expiring. Amazingly, the ball banked off the backboard and fell through the net. The clock struck zero.

Celtics win, 111–110!

The crowd rushed the court in celebration! Several players headed to the locker room in excitement . . .

but . . . but . . . the timekeeper had made a mistake! There was still one second left! The game wasn't over. A thousand fans were already on the court. One crazy fan ran to the referee Richie Powers and punched him in the face. True story!

The police had to clear the court for the game to finish. The players had to come back from the locker room.

The Suns had no time-outs, but Westphal purposely called one anyway, the penalty for which was a one-shot technical foul. He did it as a ploy to have the ball moved to half-court (instead of under the Suns' own basket, where it would have been nearly impossible to get a good look at the basket with one second left).

Jo Jo White made the free throw. 112–110, Boston. One second left.

With the court lined with fans waiting to erupt yet again for a Boston victory, Perry threw the inbound pass to Heard, who caught the ball to the right of the key, turned, and threw up a desperation, high-arching fadeaway over Nelson as time expired.

Good!

The scored was tied at 112. The fans who had so

recently stormed the court in celebration now stood dumbfounded and silent.

For all those shots against the Celtics that missed—by the Lakers in 1962, by the 76ers in 1965, by the Lakers again in 1969—and for all the times the Celtics just seemed to have luck on their side—this shot went in.

Triple overtime.

Phoenix took another lead, but this time, the Celtics' experience won the day. Boston went up 126–120 with thirty-six seconds left, but *another* Phoenix run led by Westphal nearly stole the game. *Nearly,* but not quite.

Final score: Boston 128, Phoenix 126 in triple OT.

It was over. No one had ever seen anything like it. Jo Jo White played sixty minutes and scored 33 points. The Celtics had won the greatest game ever played in the NBA Finals. Heinsohn, the Celtics coach, collapsed from exhaustion and high blood pressure.

Two days later in Phoenix, the Celtics won their thirteenth title, and Havlicek's eighth, finally putting away the tough, determined Suns, 87–80.

Even years later, when most memories of this

Finals matchup have faded, fans could never forget the adrenaline-filled ride that was Game 5. To this day, Game 5 remains one of the most amazing moments in sports history. No NBA Finals game since has topped it.

I'm not sure one ever will.

THE FINALS OF THE 1970s

TOP TEN LIST

When the pressure is on and thousands of fans are watching your every move, it takes a special player to play his best basketball at a pivotal moment. The NBA Finals is the proving ground in the NBA, where the cream of the crop distinguish themselves from the rest of the pack—here are the ten big-game players of the decade that you wanted on the court with the championship on the line.

1. Kareem Abdul-Jabbar (Milwaukee Bucks, Los Angeles Lakers): Averaged 27.0 points, 18.5 rebounds, and 2.8 assists per game in the Bucks' 1971 Finals win against the Baltimore Bullets. He returned to the Finals with the Bucks in 1974, ultimately losing to Boston, but he still posted

stellar numbers in the series: 32.6 points, 12.1 rebounds, and 5.4 assists per game.

2. Rick Barry (San Francisco Warriors, Oakland Oaks/Washington Caps, New York Nets, Golden State Warriors, Houston Rockets): Hit 30 out of 32 free throws in the 1975 Finals series against the Washington Bullets, and averaged 29.5 points per game, earning MVP honors on the way to Golden State's first-ever championship.

3. Jo Jo White (Boston Celtics, Golden State Warriors, Kansas City Kings): MVP of the 1976 Finals, Boston Celtics versus Phoenix Suns. He was the star of Game 5, the greatest Finals game ever, which was decided by two points in triple overtime, scoring a team-high 33 points.

4. Dennis Johnson (Seattle SuperSonics, Phoenix Suns, Boston Celtics): Seattle's defensive wizard and clutch offensive player who led the SuperSonics to victory against the Washington Bullets in the 1979 Finals. His 22.6 points, 6 assists, and 6 rebounds per game were MVP-worthy.

5. Wilt Chamberlain (San Francisco–Philadelphia

Warriors, Philadelphia 76ers, Los Angeles Lakers): Dominated the 1972 Finals, when the Lakers squared off against the Knicks. He averaged a whopping 23.2 rebounds per game in the Lakers' first-ever title win in Los Angeles.

6. Willis Reed (New York Knicks): Named the Finals MVP for the Knicks in 1970 and 1973, defeating the Lakers in both matchups. They were New York's first—and only—two NBA titles.

7. Bill Walton (Portland Trail Blazers, San Diego–Los Angeles Clippers, Boston Celtics): Overwhelmed the 76ers in the 1977 Finals, particularly on the offensive and defensive boards, averaging a double-double (18.5 points, 19.0 rebounds) on the way to a championship.

8. John Havlicek (Boston Celtics): Boston's consummate big-game player and MVP of the 1974 Finals versus Milwaukee. He averaged a team-high 26.4 points per game.

9. Jerry West (Los Angeles Lakers): Win or lose, "Mr. Clutch" always performed. He played in three Finals for the Lakers in the 1970s, winning one in 1972 against the Knicks. Even as he aged,

he remained a top scorer, averaging 31.3, 19.8, and 21.4 points per game from the ages of 31 to 34.

10. Walt Frazier (New York Knicks, Cleveland Cavaliers): Scored 36 points in a stirring Game 7 of the 1970 Finals against the Lakers. The Knicks legend finished with averages of 17.6 points, 7.7 rebounds, and 10.4 assists in the series.

THE
1980s

THE STORY
OF THE 1980s

THE REBIRTH:
CELTICS VS. LAKERS

y 1980, the NBA had to admit it was in real
trouble. So many conversations that had
taken place within the league were now public issues.

In the 1940s, basketball, just like the other sports
and much of society, was segregated. Basketball was
largely a white game in the Midwest and a Jewish
game in East Coast cities. The first black players
entered the league in 1950, but in many ways, the
number of African American players was controlled
by coaches and executives. Though the game exploded
in popularity in African American neighborhoods,

NBA basketball in the 1960s was still a largely white or evenly mixed game racially. It wasn't until the mid-1960s that the Boston Celtics became the first team to play five African Americans on the court at the same time.

By the 1970s, the NBA grew into a game predominately played by African Americans, both statistically and stylistically, especially in the ABA. The strict, slow, game of rigid fundamentals gave way to creative athleticism. And America was changing, in part because basketball's popularity among youth was growing. Once, only a few players, like Bill Russell, Elgin Baylor, and Wilt Chamberlain, had dominated above the rim. Now the game was being played almost exclusively in the air. Believe it or not, at one point coaches *hated* slam dunks. Now dunks were an awesome part of the game in the eyes of coaches, fans, and players. Though the ABA had folded in 1976, so much of the league's fast and free style was adopted in the NBA, including the three-point shot, which was added to the NBA in 1979.

The game was more exciting and fun, the players more gifted—but there was a problem: the league's ratings were low on television. Everyone knew that the great, dominant Celtics in their best years still couldn't draw ten thousand fans per night. It would be unthinkable today that fans wouldn't want to watch Kobe Bryant or LeBron James or Kevin Durant, but thirty-five years ago, it was true: Fans weren't sure the NBA was worth it. Even the playoffs and NBA Finals weren't shown on live TV nationally.

Some fans believed that NBA players didn't care enough to play hard for the entire game. For all the thrills and dunks and unbelievable athletic moves, a mean joke became popular about the NBA: viewers only had to watch the final five minutes of a game to see the whole thing.

Worse was the idea among television executives that the NBA had too many African American players, many of whom played "selfish basketball."

As if the NBA didn't already have enough of an image problem, several high-profile incidents of cocaine use by star players came to light, giving the impression that the league also had a rampant drug problem.

Something had to change.

And by the most amazing happenstance, a sort of miracle occurred.

There was a kid out of Lansing, Michigan, who played basketball with a combination of joy and competitiveness the league had never seen before. Usually if a player smiled too much, most people thought he was not serious about winning—but not this kid. He was tall, six foot nine—the tallest point guard in the history of the league—yet could dribble and pass and control the pace and tempo of the game like no one his height ever had before.

His name was Earvin Johnson, and he did so many magical things with the basketball that his nickname was, appropriately, Magic.

One state over, in French Lick, Indiana, there was another kid, three years older. Same height as Magic, six foot nine. If Magic Johnson could pass like nobody six nine ever could before, this kid from Indiana could *shoot* like no one his height ever could before. His name was Larry Bird.

Magic smiled and hugged on the court. Bird played with a grim fierceness, as though he had something to prove each time he had the ball. Magic was black. Bird was white. Both understood the way basketball should be played, as a team game where scoring was just one part of it.

In a time of terrific athleticism, neither could run or jump like Dr. J or was a super-dunker like Dominique Wilkins, whose nickname, "The Human Highlight Film," tells you all you need to know. Bird and Magic played the game, instead, with near-perfect pass-first, unselfish fundamentals. And both had a habit of winning.

Amazingly, they were rivals before even entering the league. Each remained in state for college—Johnson for the Big Ten Michigan State Spartans, Bird for the little-known Indiana State Sycamores. Powerhouse or underdog, it didn't matter. Johnson and Bird ended up playing each other for the national championship. Magic's Michigan State team beat Bird's undefeated Indiana State team, 75–64.

The next year, 1979, they wound up on the two most historic teams in the league: Bird to Boston and Magic to Los Angeles.

Most important: Both delivered. Larry Bird and Magic Johnson were so good they saved the NBA.

Think about that: They reinvigorated an entire sport in America.

What followed next was the greatest decade the league had ever seen, and it is the reason the NBA is as cool and popular and fun as it is today. The 1980s exploded from the start. It was basketball paradise, where teams were just as important as individuals. The Lakers already had All-Star Kareem Abdul-Jabbar at center, but with the youthful, exuberant Magic Johnson taking on the point guard role, the giant with the unstoppable skyhook was revived. Kareem won the league MVP, and the Lakers won the NBA title in 1980, Magic's rookie season.

Bird and Magic. Magic won the championship in his rookie season, but Bird was the Rookie of the Year. Bird won the championship in his second year, Magic in the third. Bird won three straight Most Valuable Player Awards from 1984 to 1986, and during that time was lifted into the conversation as being perhaps the greatest player who ever lived. Then Magic won three MVP trophies as well, in 1987, 1989, and 1990. The league's two greatest teams, Boston and Los Angeles, with its two greatest players, Magic and Bird, made the NBA the hottest league in the 1980s.

In between Los Angeles and Boston was Philadelphia. In between Magic and Bird was the great Dr. J. Philadelphia had already been championship material before the arrival of Magic and Bird, and with the addition in 1982 of league MVP Moses Malone to play center, the league now had three powerhouse franchises, all of them with superstars and all already renowned in NBA history.

The 1980s in the NBA were special for multiple reasons, and one of the most important was this: The great rivalries of the 1960s were reborn. Boston versus Philadelphia, formerly with the marquee matchup of Bill Russell versus Wilt Chamberlain, was revived in this new era through the rivalry of Bird versus Dr. J. Boston versus Los Angeles? Again, Russell versus Wilt, reborn as Magic versus Bird. The NBA's classic roots were pulled into the modern day, with a new generation of players filling historic roles in great sports cities.

The big three of Boston, Philadelphia, and LA would utterly dominate the '80s. At least one of the three would appear in the NBA Finals every year of the decade—and the eventual champion came from this special group of three teams NINE out of the ten years. That is dominance.

The 1980s represented the years when both individual talent and team identification were at their highest and most even. The decade was filled with superstars and characters. It was a decade-long talent show. In the East, Philadelphia was on top when Bird arrived. The Celtics had to overcome Philadelphia, which they did after the 1983 season, to become the dominant team in the conference.

Another great team of the decade, the Milwaukee Bucks, had the task of overcoming Philadelphia *and* Boston. Yet for all their excellence, the Bucks couldn't get past the 76ers or the Celtics, and would go down as one of the best, most forgotten teams in NBA history.

Only the Detroit Pistons, led by Isiah Thomas and his soon-to-be nicknamed "Bad Boys," were able to break up the party, capturing the title in the final year of the decade, 1989.

The '80s would deliver a slew of stars to fans, well beyond the dynamic duo of Bird and Magic. Ever hear of Michael Jordan? Hakeem Olajuwon, Patrick Ewing, and Charles Barkley? All were stars in the '80s, year in and year out.

Jordan and the rest of the Bulls had assumed the position the Pistons had once occupied: the team that had to prove it could beat the top dogs before calling itself one as well. Though they made life tough for the best of teams, the Bulls wouldn't break through and win it all until the 1990–91 season.

By the end of the '80s, the league was not only back but more powerful and more popular than ever. Boston was back. The Lakers were back. The big cities—Chicago with Jordan, New York with Ewing—were rising with star players. By the close of the decade, the league that at one time hadn't been able to get its championship games on prime-time television had *expanded* to Miami and Orlando, where a new giant who wore a size-22 sneaker (yes, 22!), Shaquille O'Neal, would arrive a few years later. On the brink of disaster to start the decade, the NBA was now on the brink of a worldwide explosion no one could have imagined.

THE STORY OF THE 1980s

TOP TEN LIST

Throughout the history of the NBA, the league has continually transformed, undergoing many changes, most of which remain in effect today, though others have been left behind. Perhaps the greatest number of changes in the league occurred in the 1980s—here are ten ways the NBA evolved during the decade.

1. Three to make two: The NBA created (and then quickly eliminated) a new rule that allowed players to shoot three foul shots to make two when the opposing team was over the team foul limit. It didn't last long because it made free-throw shooting too easy.

2. Expanded playoff series: The first round of the playoffs expanded from a best

two-of-three format to a best three-of-five series.

3. Adios, Kansas City: The Kings moved from Kansas City to Sacramento in 1985.

4. Welcome, Dallas: The Dallas Mavericks franchise was born at the start of the 1980–81 season, becoming the twenty-third team in the league.

5. 2-3-2: The best-of-seven Finals format switched to a 2-3-2 format in 1985, meaning the first two games of the series would now be played on the court of the team with home-court advantage, the middle three games would be played at the other team's home court, and the final two games (if necessary) would also be played at the home-court advantage team's court. The rule was changed again in the 2014–15 season to a 2-2-1-1-1 format.

6. More expansion: The Miami Heat were formed in 1988 and the Orlando Magic in 1989.

7. Adios, New Orleans: The Jazz moved from New Orleans to Utah in 1979.

8. Bonus ball: The three-point shot was adopted in the 1979–80 season, though it was first instituted in the ABA before the two leagues merged.

9. All-Star Weekend: The Slam Dunk and Three-Point contests were added to All-Star Weekend.

10. Trading places: At the start of 1980, Houston and San Antonio moved to the Western Conference, and Chicago and Milwaukee moved to the Eastern.

THE PLAYERS OF THE 1980s

The 1980s brought about a resurgence in popularity for the NBA, led by the great rivalry between Larry Bird and Magic Johnson. Yet there were other individual players who brought their own brand of flash and helped make the 1980s a glorious moment in professional basketball history. You might be familiar with one of those other players. He goes by the name of Michael Jordan. Including Jordan, here is a list of five players who defined the decade.

MICHAEL JORDAN
Years: 1984–1993, 1995–1998, 2001–2003
Position: Guard
Height: 6 ft. 6 in.

Teams: Chicago Bulls (1984–1993, 1995–1998), Washington Wizards (2001–2003)

Championships: 6 (1991, 1992, 1993, 1996, 1997, 1998 Bulls)

Most Valuable Player Awards: 5 (1988, 1991, 1992, 1996, 1998)

Jersey Number: 12 (Chicago), 23 (Chicago, Washington), 45 (Chicago)

Nicknames: MJ, Air Jordan, His Airness

All-Star Games: 14

Hall of Fame: 2009

He was always different, this Michael Jordan. They said he wasn't big enough to play on his high school varsity team, which fueled an already-hungry kid. Years later, that hungry kid was proving his doubters dead wrong, playing as a freshman at one of the greatest colleges (University of North Carolina) under one of the greatest coaches (Dean Smith), capping off his first season by hitting the game-winning shot in the 1982 NCAA Men's Basketball national championship. By the time he was drafted third in the 1984 NBA draft by the Chicago Bulls, Michael Jordan had grown to six foot six.

Jordan won a college championship and an Olympic gold medal in 1984. Then he took the NBA by storm. In college, Jordan had been athletic and exciting, and it'd been obvious he was going to be an excellent player. But Coach Smith's slow-paced style plus the zone defenses colleges could employ (zone defenses were illegal in the NBA) had hidden what Michael Jordan could really do on a basketball court. When Jordan arrived in the NBA, where defenses were forced to play him man-to-man, he soared.

Immediately, Jordan became Elgin Baylor and Julius Erving all in one. He leaped. He flew. He dunked. Erving was graceful with occasional power. Jordan was a power dunker with grace. He was a better outside shooter than the Doctor, and within months, the world knew Michael Jordan was a special player at the highest level.

Everything about Jordan was different, as though his movements created a movement. It started with the sneakers. All the greats wore them, but Jordan had his own, Air Jordans, which created a billion-dollar sneaker industry. For decades, basketball shorts were so short and so tight they looked like swimming trunks. Jordan's shorts were longer, and another style trend was created. Michael Jordan shaved his head, so everybody shaved their heads.

In the 1980s, Jordan scored and scored and scored, but it was in his second year, in the 1986 best-of-five playoffs against Boston, that Jordan gave a glimpse of what he could become. Before then, he expressed great frustration that he was a showstopper whose teams couldn't win. Once, he said, "Fans want to come watch me score forty points and see their team win."

Earlier in the year, he had injured his foot and missed half the season. The Bulls had still qualified for the playoffs against Larry Bird and the powerful Celtics, and the Bulls' doctors had advised Jordan not to play.

Jordan would have none of it.

In the first game, matched up against Boston's Dennis Johnson, who was considered one of the best defensive guards of all time and was once the MVP of the NBA Finals in 1979, Jordan put up 49 points. He hit from inside, outside, mid-range. On one defensive switch, he was matched up against Bird. Jordan put the ball between his legs once, twice, three times, backed into the great Bird and then spun around to the baseline for a jumper.

But the Celtics won.

In Game 2, a Sunday afternoon at Boston Garden, Jordan was even better. No, he was the *best ever*. Dunk after jumper, shot after free throw, the Celtics couldn't guard him. No combination could stop Jordan. The Celtics thought they had won the game in regulation, but Celtics power forward Kevin McHale was called for a foul. Jordan hit both free throws to force overtime. In OT, Jordan had his easiest shot of the afternoon, a wide-open 15-footer . . . but he missed.

Double overtime.

When it was over, the Celtics escaped 135–131, but Jordan had given the basketball world something it would never forget. He finished with 63 points, the most points in a playoff game ever, surpassing that night in Boston Garden back in 1962, when Elgin Baylor had scored 61 for the Lakers in Game 5 of the NBA Finals.

The Celtics won the series two nights later in Chicago. Jordan would score just 19 points, and the rest of the decade would follow the same pattern: Jordan would be spectacular individually, scoring points and dazzling crowds and building the NBA to a level of popularity even higher than Magic and Bird had, but the better teams of his time—the Celtics, Pistons, and Lakers—were always the winners.

Michael Jordan vowed to change this, and he kept his promise. As you'll find out in the 1990s chapters, in the following decade, he would become the greatest winner since Bill Russell.

MOSES MALONE
Years: 1974–1994
Position: Center
Height: 6 ft. 10 in.
Teams: Utah Stars (ABA, 1974–1975), Spirits of St. Louis (1975–1976), Buffalo Braves (1976), Houston Rockets (1976–1982), Philadelphia 76ers (1982–1986, 1993), Washington Bullets (1986–1988), Atlanta Hawks (1988–1991), Milwaukee Bucks (1991–1993), San Antonio Spurs (1994–1995)
Championships: 1 (1983 76ers)
Most Valuable Player Awards: 3 (1979, 1982, 1983)
Jersey Number: 22 (Utah), 13 (St. Louis), 20 (Buffalo), 21 (Houston), 24 (Houston),

2 (Philadelphia, Atlanta, San Antonio), 4
Washington), 8 Milwaukee)
Nickname: Chairman of the Boards
All-Star Games: 13 (1 ABA, 12 NBA)
Hall of Fame: 2001

Tireless, relentless, unstoppable. Those are the words
that best described Moses Malone, one of the great
and most underrated players in history.

Beyond all his spectacular talent, Moses was a legend for three specific reasons.

1. He was one of the first players in history to jump
   straight from high school to the pros.
2. In a game dominated by seven-foot centers
   like Wilt Chamberlain, then Kareem Abdul-
   Jabbar and Bill Walton, Moses was six ten and
   became the most dominant center in the game,
   taking that title for a time even from the great
   Abdul-Jabbar.
3. His arrival in Philadelphia ended years
   of frustration and brought the 76ers a
   championship.

Before the 2006 draft, when the rule that forced
players to wait one year after high school before

going to the NBA went into effect, players routinely entered the league from high school because they felt their talent was good enough to forgo college. For example, Kobe Bryant never went to college, and neither did Kevin Garnett nor LeBron James. In the 1970s, however, the only players who were allowed to skip college and go straight to the pros were called "hardship cases," meaning that a player had to prove hardship—such as difficult family financial circumstances—to be allowed to enter the NBA. Moses was one of the first, but the NBA wouldn't allow his petition for early entry, so he joined the ABA's Utah Stars. After the ABA and NBA merged in 1976, Malone ended up on the Buffalo Braves (now the Los Angeles Clippers), but he was then traded to the Houston Rockets after two games.

At six foot ten, 250 pounds, Moses was a terrific rebounder on defense, but he was also a one-man show on the offensive boards. A shot would go up, and Moses would tip it, tip it again, and finally catch it, take the ball from his opponents, and score. His rebounding ability allowed him to be a great scorer as well—Malone finished his career with 29,580 points, putting him at seventh all-time.

Moses was not a pretty basketball player: He became great by working his butt off, every shot, every rebound, every day. People would say Moses could get more offensive rebounds on one trip down-court than most other players would in a whole game. Rebounding is about desire, and Moses was hungrier. Rightfully so, he earned the nickname "Chairman of the Boards" for his incredible ability to rebound. His style of tipping the ball to himself was a nifty trick that helped him get around a weakness of his: Although he was nearly seven feet tall, Moses's hands were so small that he couldn't palm a basketball, making it difficult for him to immediately control the ball on a rebound. Throughout his career, he led the league in rebounding six times, including a streak of five seasons in a row, and he ranks third all-time in total rebounds, finishing his career with 17,834.

When he joined the NBA Houston Rockets, Malone took off. He won the NBA MVP in 1979. Then in 1981, the Rockets made the playoffs with a weak 40-42 record. But even a weak record doesn't change the fact that as long as you make it to the playoffs, you get a shot to win it all.

Moses got hot in the playoffs, upset Magic Johnson,

Kareem, and the defending-champion Lakers in the first round, and Houston became the only team in NBA history to reach the NBA Finals with a losing record. They played Larry Bird's Celtics, who beat them in six hard games.

Moses won another MVP in 1982 with Houston and then became the missing piece to Philadelphia's championship aspirations when the Rockets traded him to the 76ers. With Dr. J, Andrew Toney, and Malone, the 76ers were for one year the most dominant team in the league, winning the title in 1983.

In a terrible trade, Malone was sent to Washington in 1986 and was never quite as good as he'd been with Houston and Philly, but for those who saw him in his prime, his act in the 1980s was hard to top.

ISIAH THOMAS
Years: 1981–1994
Position: Point Guard
Height: 6 ft. 1 in.
Team: Detroit Pistons
Championships: 2 (1989, 1990 Pistons)
Most Valuable Player Awards: 0
Jersey Number: 11

Nickname: Zeke

All-Star Games: 12

Hall of Fame: 2000

There were all kinds of things that people said about Isiah Thomas. He was called the "Baby-Faced Assassin" because, according to the *Charlotte Observer*, an opposing coach once said of Thomas, "He smiles at you, then cuts you down." He was called the most dominant six-foot-one-inch player in the history of the game. He was called "Zeke." He was hated in Boston. He was hated in New York. He was hated in Chicago, even though it was his hometown. He was hated in all these places because he was the engine that allowed the Detroit Pistons by the end of the 1980s to take down the Celtics and the Lakers, and to keep the emerging Michael Jordan from winning as well as scoring points.

But Isiah was beloved in Detroit, where the Pistons drafted him after his Indiana Hoosiers won the NCAA title in 1981. Thomas went pro after only two years at Indiana and was an instant NBA sensation.

Until Allen Iverson and Steph Curry came along, few players could rival Isiah's dribble, which was equally amazing with his right or left hand. He could dribble on the run at full speed, changing hands and direction without slowing down. He could dribble full speed, stop, and nail a jumper at the foul line. Like the great Tiny Archibald before him, Isiah could score like a shooting guard but still run an offense like a classic point guard.

There was no one like him. Scoring point guards, who looked to shoot first, usually wound up being ball hogs who forgot that a point guard's job is to control the offense and help their teammates find opportunities to score. Isiah rebuffed that old way of thinking, showing fans that pure passing points guards didn't have the offensive firepower to carry their teams the way he could. That isn't to say he couldn't dish it like the best of 'em—Isiah was an assists machine, ranking seventh all time in the category.

What truly defined Isiah's game, however, was his toughness. He was considered a "little guy," but he backed down from no one, like in the 1984 playoffs when he and Bernard King of the Knicks put on a scoring show in the climactic Game 5. Isiah scored 16 points in a row down the stretch even though Detroit lost the series. He didn't back down from the Celtics, or the Lakers, or the Sixers.

In the 1987 Eastern Conference finals, the Pistons (whose nickname was "the Bad Boys") were out to prove they were just as good as, if not better than, the Celtics. But Thomas, the man who led the offense with a rare sense of mastery, made the worst mistake of his career, allowing Larry Bird to steal his inbounds pass, turning a potential stunning Game 5 win in Boston into a painful defeat. The Celtics won the series in seven hard games.

It was a temporary blip, as Detroit dethroned Boston the next year and reached the Finals. Despite Thomas's brilliance on the court in the series, high-lighted by his Game 6 performance, in which he scored 25 points in a single quarter, an NBA Finals record, the Pistons lost to the Lakers in a seven-game Finals.

Out for revenge the following season, Detroit beat LA in the 1989 Finals. The Pistons won another title the season after, and Isiah was named the Finals MVP.

Thomas's excellence was enshrined in 2000, when he was named to the Hall of Fame in his first year of eligibility. Isiah Thomas was the greatest thing ever to happen to Detroit basketball, and to this day, Thomas is the Pistons' all-time leader in points, assists, and steals. Isiah put Detroit basketball on the map, and the team has never been as good as during his glory days.

GEORGE GERVIN

Years: 1972–1986

Position: Shooting guard–small forward

Height: 6 ft. 7 in.

Teams: Virginia Squires (ABA, 1972–1974), San Antonio Spurs (ABA, 1974–1976, NBA 1977–1985), Chicago Bulls (1985–1986)

Championships: 0

Most Valuable Player Awards: 0

Jersey Number: 44 (Virginia, San Antonio), 8 (Chicago)

Nicknames: Ice, Iceman

All-Star Games: 12 (3 ABA, 9 NBA)

Hall of Fame: 1996

"The Iceman" kind of says it all because George Gervin was cool. He was one of the great scoring machines of his time. Both in the ABA and the NBA, the Iceman was the first name in points.

He was skinny as a rail, six seven but only 185 pounds. Gervin's game was artistic, creative, and always improvisational. He could shoot with either hand but was predominantly right-handed. He was known for his baseline drives that often ended not with a dunk but a pretty finger roll a few feet from the hoop.

Gervin was an unlikely scorer because he was so slight yet constantly attacked the basket. He was not a three-point shooter but the kind of player who always found a way, whether with layups, jumpers, floaters, runners, or free throws, to score points.

Gervin was another classic scorer who shot a lot. Ten times he ranked in the top seven in the league in shots attempted but shot 50 percent from the field for his career. Gervin was also a tremendous foul shooter. Four times he led the league in scoring.

One of those scoring titles came in the 1978 season. Going into the final game of the year, Gervin was neck and neck with David Thompson, the Denver Nuggets' star scorer, for the title. Thompson had already dropped an astounding 73 points in his final game to take a slight lead over Gervin. Gervin needed 58 points to win the scoring title.

What ensued was one of the greatest offensive performances in the history of the game. Gervin started off cold, but then he heated up and heated up some more until he was officially *red hot*.

In his final game of the season, Thompson had broken the record for most points scored in a single quarter (32). The record stood for only a handful of hours. Gervin scored 20 points in the first quarter and proceeded to tally a whopping *33* in the second quarter, breaking Thompson's record! (Another Thompson, the Warriors' Klay Thompson, broke Gervin's record in 2015.)

With 53 points at half, Gervin had no trouble adding 10 more points in the third quarter, bringing his total to 63, earning him the scoring title. Gervin sat out the end of the third quarter and all of the fourth quarter to rest, leaving fans wondering how high he could've gone if he'd been given the chance.

As much as Gervin was a legend, an offensive genius and fan favorite with his odd, slingshot shooting motion, Gervin never reached the Finals. His Spurs teams in the 1980s were talented but never quite good enough to challenge the Lakers. Gervin, of course, could score against anyone, averaging 26.5 points in the playoffs for his career, and would one day be inducted into the basketball Hall of Fame, but the one area he was never known for—defense—might also be the reason he never won a championship. Still, the Iceman was something to see.

BERNARD KING

Years: 1977–1993

Position: Shooting guard–small forward

Height: 6 ft. 7 in.

Teams: New Jersey Nets (1977–1979, 1992), Utah Jazz (1979), Golden State Warriors (1980–1982), New York Knicks (1982–1987), Washington Bullets (1988–1991)

Championships: 0

Most Valuable Player Awards: 0

Jersey Number: 22 (New Jersey, Utah), 30 (Golden State, New York, Washington, New Jersey)

Nicknames: B, the King

All-Star Games: 4

Hall of Fame: 2013

Few players captured the hearts of their home fans like Bernard King, one of the most devastating scorers in the history of the game. King was a comet, whose greatness flashed across the NBA sky in the 1980s, and in the years he was healthy and mentally and emotionally fit, NBA teams on a nightly basis had to deal with the one of the most explosive players ever to hold a basketball.

After a glorious career at the University of Tennessee, King was drafted by the New Jersey Nets, who were expecting greatness and got it. King averaged 24.2 and 21.6 points per game in his first two seasons, but then he was traded to Utah, not because of his playing but because of his alcohol addiction. He played only nineteen games for the Jazz before entering a treatment facility. At the time, it appeared that one of the great promising careers was going to be ruined by drinking before it even really began.

King returned a season later, joining Golden State, and for two years recaptured the scoring touch he'd had when he'd first entered the league. But it wasn't until he joined the Knicks in 1982 that Bernard King really took off.

Today, fans are used to teams shooting three-pointers routinely, but King was nearly a 30-point scorer on average *without* the long ball, and shot for a high percentage, well over 50 percent. His patented shot was a turnaround jumper, which he could get off against even much taller opponents because of his quick release. King was also a speedy player who could score on the fast break.

The 1983–84 playoffs was Bernard King at his best. No one could stop him. Not the rising Detroit Pistons, against whom King outdueled a young Isiah Thomas in a five-game classic. Part of what made it a classic was that King had dislocated *both* of his middle fingers and still played with his middle and ring fingers taped together on his shooting hand. And man, did King come to *play*.

King averaged 42.6 points for the series. The Knicks won the first game by a point, 94–93. King scored 36. Detroit won Game 2, but King scored 46 of New York's 105 points. King scored 46 again in Game 3, 41 in Game 4, and 44 in a 127–123 overtime win in the deciding Game 5.

In the second round, King met the mighty Boston Celtics. Both forwards Kevin McHale and Cedric Maxwell vowed King was finished. Nobody would dominate the great Celtics.

But King wasn't finished. The Celtics won the first

two games at home, but King scored 24, 43, and 44 points in the Knicks' home games, which brought the series to a deciding seventh game in Boston. The Celtics were too much in the end. Larry Bird scored 39 to King's 24, and the Celtics won the series, but those twelve Bernard King playoff games were truly memorable.

Then disaster struck. In 1985, King shattered his leg in a game against Sacramento and missed the entire 1986 season. After he recovered from the injury, he was never the same explosive, dominant player he'd been before. Injuries would eat away at the great King, but New York fans never forgot the glory days of Bernard King, like the time he scored 50 points two nights in a row. Neither did the league, which inducted him into the Hall of Fame in 2013.

THE PLAYERS OF THE 1980s
TOP TEN LIST

Earvin "Magic" Johnson played a major role in putting the NBA on the map and making it one of the most popular professional sports leagues in the world—and it didn't hurt that he had a cool nickname to go along with his basketball skills. But Magic isn't the only player around with a stylish nickname. Here are some of the greatest nicknames from 1960 to 1990.

1. Chocolate Thunder: Philadelphia's Darryl Dawkins, who gave the nickname to himself for his imposing presence and dunks so powerful he even shattered a backboard!

2. Skywalker: Denver Nuggets guard-forward David Thompson's incredible jumping ability was the source of his nickname—Thompson was one

of the first players to utilize the alley-oop dunk.

3. The Microwave: Detroit Pistons guard Vinnie Johnson was known for scoring often, in quick bursts, and earned a reputation because "he heats up fast."

4. The Mailman: Utah Jazz forward Karl Malone was one of the most consistent players in league history, causing many to say "he always delivers."

5. The Iceman: San Antonio Spurs guard-forward George Gervin was known for his *cool*, calm, and collected attitude on the court.

6. Clyde: New York Knicks guard Walt Frazier, famous for his flamboyant fashion sense, wore a wide-brimmed fedora hat similar to the one worn by the character Clyde Barrow (played by the actor Warren Beatty) in the famous movie *Bonnie and Clyde*.

7. Human Highlight Film: Atlanta Hawks forward and slam dunk machine Dominique Wilkins produced highlight-worthy dunk after highlight-worthy dunk throughout his career.

8. The Chief: Boston Celtics center Robert Parish was so stoic on the court his teammate Cedric

Maxwell (number ten on this list) started calling Parish "Chief" after the fictitious Chief Bromden, a silent Native American character in the classic movie *One Flew Over the Cuckoo's Nest*.

9. Dr. Dunkenstein: Utah Jazz guard Darrell Griffith's amazing leaping abilities made him one of the best—and fiercest—dunkers in the NBA.

10. Cornbread: Boston Celtics forward Cedric Maxwell was once told by college teammate Melvin Watkins that he looked like the main character in the 1975 film *Cornbread, Earl and Me*. Needless to say, the name stuck.

THE FINALS
OF THE 1980s

1984: BOSTON CELTICS VS.
LOS ANGELES LAKERS

I t was a Finals series that had been years in the making.

Finally, this was it: Celtics versus Lakers. Larry Bird versus Magic Johnson. They hadn't met for a championship since their epic Indiana State–Michigan State NCAA championship game in 1979. Magic had been the victor in that matchup. Either Magic or Bird had been in the NBA Finals every year since they entered the league in 1980. The Lakers had been to the Finals six times since 1970, winning three championships. The Celtics had made it three times, winning all three. Yet Boston and Los

Angeles hadn't faced each other in the playoffs since 1969.

The 1984 Celtics were motivated. The year before, they'd been swept out of the playoffs by Milwaukee, losing four straight, the first time a Celtics team had been swept in a best-of-seven series ever. Afterward, they hired a new coach, Celtics legend K. C. Jones, the Hall of Fame guard who'd won eight championships with the Celtics. The Lakers were motivated, too, having been swept away in the Finals the year before by Moses Malone and the 76ers. The Celtics had faced the Magic Johnson Lakers in the past, but in Game 1 of the 1984 Finals, they looked like a JV team going against the varsity squad. Magic was too good. The Lakers' speed was too much. It wasn't just Magic, but also shooting guard Byron Scott and power forward James Worthy who ran past Boston. The Celtics at one point were down 32–12. Boston fans looked at each other with fear, bewilderment, and one thought:

How are we gonna win a game against these guys?

The Celtics *would* make a comeback—but it wouldn't be enough.

Game 1: Lakers 115, Celtics 109.

Game 2: This one was a closer, more competitive

game than Game 1, but the Lakers still looked just a notch better, and they held a 113–111 lead with eighteen seconds left. Magic inbounded to Worthy, who floated a weak pass crosscourt. Celtics backup guard Gerald Henderson stole the ball in midair and scored to tie it with thirteen seconds left. Then Magic made his first mistake of the Finals, taking too much time and dribbling out the clock with the game still tied.

The Celtics had new life, and they used it. After building a slim lead in overtime, Robert Parish, the great Boston center, stripped Kareem Abdul-Jabbar of the ball to seal the win, 124–121 (OT). The series was headed west to California tied, 1-1. If the Celtics thought the Lakers were great in Game 1, the Lakers were even better at home in Game 3, running down the middle, passing, dunking, scoring at will. Magic Johnson set an NBA Finals record with 21 assists. The Celtics did not fight hard enough, Bird said. He called his team "sissies." To get beat by 33 points was unacceptable. But that's what happened. Lakers 137, Celtics 104.

Game 4 was the game that changed the series. Until this point, the 1984 Finals had been played completely on the Lakers' terms. The Celtics had allowed them to run, especially on the fast break, and score in the open court. Then, in the third quarter, LA power forward Kurt Rambis raced to the hoop for another fast break layup. This time, however, Celtics power forward Kevin McHale fouled Rambis around his neck, tackling him to the floor. The message was sent to the flashy Lakers: no more easy baskets. The Celtics were going to play tough. McHale and Rambis had to be separated. Later, Kareem threw an elbow at Bird, and the two nearly got into a fight. The Celtics had turned the Finals into a street fight, and it worked. Bird led the way for the Celtics with 29 points, and Parish added another 25. Final score: Celtics 129, Lakers 125 (OT). The series was tied at two games apiece.

Game 5 would forever be known as the "heat game." Why? The temperature inside the ancient Boston Garden was almost 100 degrees (it had no air conditioning). One of the referees became so dehydrated that he fainted! The conditions may have been brutal, but Larry Bird still found a way to look fresh. He dominated, scoring 34 points and grabbing 17 rebounds. And the Celtics kept their momentum going with a relatively easy 121–103 win to take a 3-2 series lead.

Boston went back to LA for Game 6 ready to close out the series and secure their title. It was another physical contest, with hard fouls and a shoving match between James Worthy and Celtics small forward Cedric Maxwell. Bird was terrific again, falling two assists shy of a triple-double. But Abdul-Jabbar and Magic Johnson took advantage of a boisterous home crowd to lead the Lakers to a 119–108 win. Abdul-Jabbar had 30 points and 10 rebounds. The series was now tied, 3-3.

That left Game 7. Winner-take-all one more time between these two legendary teams. The teams once again traveled cross-country to the Boston Garden. Electric fans were brought in to cool the air. The temperature may have been better, but the playing was not. The game was tense. The Celtics didn't shoot well, but Maxwell told the team, "Get on my back, boys. I'll carry you." The man nicknamed "Cornbread" wasn't kidding; he would go on to score 24 points to lead the team, with eight rebounds and eight assists. The Celtics held a double-digit lead near the end of the game, but the Lakers fought back and narrowed the gap to three in the final minutes. But that was as close as LA would come. Abdul-Jabbar's game-high 29 points weren't enough to counter a balanced Celtics scoring attack that included two additional 20-point performances behind Maxwell. But perhaps the most important statistic of the day was the rebounding edge, 52–33 in favor of Boston. Toughness was the difference.

The final score? Celtics 111, Lakers 102.

It was the fifteenth time the Celtics were champions and the eighth time they had beaten the Lakers in the Finals. Larry Bird was named MVP of the series. The Celtics had turned the series around by playing physical and crashing the boards.

Yet even so, Lakers coach Pat Riley knew what everyone who saw the series knew: Los Angeles was the better team. He reminded them about the importance of rebounding with a single phrase, "No rebound, no ring." He told his team they could never again be pushed around by Boston. And they never were. The two teams would meet twice more in the decade, in 1985 and 1987, with the Celtics being defending champions both times, and each time the Lakers won, finally dominating the team that had tormented their franchise for nearly thirty years.

1988: Los Angeles Lakers vs. Detroit Pistons

No team had won back-to-back NBA titles since Boston beat the Lakers in the famous 1969 Finals. During that time, only five defending champions—the 1973 Lakers, 1979 Bullets, 1983 Lakers, 1985 and 1987 Celtics—had even gotten *back* to the Finals for a chance to defend.

In the 1988 Finals, the Lakers were back. They were older. Kareem Abdul-Jabbar was forty years old, but LA was still gunning for their fifth title of the decade. They had avenged their bitter loss to the Celtics in 1984 by soundly beating Boston in 1985 and again in 1987.

At the championship parade after the win in '87, Lakers coach Pat Riley had said, "And we're gonna win it again next year!" The crowd, of course, went crazy.

Nearly a year later, Riley and the Lakers *were* back in the Finals. The same couldn't be said of the Boston Celtics. The Celtics were done in by age, tragedy (Len

Bias, the second overall pick in the 1986 draft, died of a cocaine overdose) and better competition, and finally beaten in the East by the rising Detroit Pistons. The Pistons had a nickname that they wore with pride: the "Bad Boys." They'd earned it due to their fierce, physical defensive style of play that many people in the NBA thought was actually *too* aggressive. The Pistons were a tough team from a tough city and if the rest of the league thought they played dirty, they didn't care.

The Pistons were led by Isiah Thomas, the lightning-quick guard who played with fearlessness and heart every night. Isiah was the visible leader, the star, but his backcourt mate, Joe Dumars, was just as tough and smart. Dumars and Thomas immediately formed one of the greatest backcourts in the league, aided by sharpshooting reserve Vinnie Johnson, whose nickname was "The Microwave" because he heated up offensively so fast. The center was Bill Laimbeer, who was known around the league as a dirty player. Laimbeer enjoyed getting other players mad, throwing them off their games, causing them to commit fouls and get distracted. Laimbeer's goal was to have his opponent concentrate on him instead of concentrating on winning. Laimbeer simply had a knack for getting under another player's skin. Boston's respected Hall of Fame center, Robert Parish, had actually punched Laimbeer in the face during the 1987 playoffs. Laimbeer was an antagonist, but his talent went beyond his ability to frustrate opponents. He was also a strong rebounder and outside shooter.

The forwards were high-scoring Adrian Dantley and bruiser Rick Mahorn, another hard-nosed guy many players in the league thought played dirty.

The Pistons were intimidators, no question about it. They would knock down the star players in the league as quickly as the guys with lesser reputations, but they weren't just enforcers. They were hungry and fierce and youthful. They had a reserve power forward named Dennis Rodman who could run and rebound all day while guarding the opposition's best player. Rodman bothered the league's best scorers, even Bird and Michael Jordan.

And this was the season the Pistons finally got past their nemesis, the Celtics. They upset the number-one-ranked team from Boston in the Eastern Conference finals and found themselves facing the Lakers, hoping to bring Detroit its first-ever NBA championship.

The Bad Boys' bruising defense was on full display in the opener from LA. Detroit smothered the Lakers, beating them by 12. It was an all-around efort as every starter and one reserve—Rodman—contributed on offense.

Determined to split their initial home stretch and avoid going down 2-0, three Lakers—Worthy, Scott, and Magic—put up twenty plus points and helped their team tie the series at one apiece.

Two games in, each team had won one game by a double-digit margin. It was a theme that would continue in Detroit for Games 3, 4, and 5. The Lakers took control of the series at first, winning Game 3 by 13 behind Magic Johnson's 18 points and 14 assists. What made Magic's performance even more impressive was the fact that he had been experiencing symptoms of the flu. Looking at his play on the court and the box score after the game, you would've never known.

The Pistons showed their toughness, though, winning Games 4 and 5. Game 4 was simply a blowout—no other way to describe it. The Pistons took an early lead and never looked back, playing aggressively on both sides of the court on their way to a 25-point victory. Then, in Game 5, Detroit looked to pick up from where they'd left off but got off to a rocky start. This time, it was the Lakers playing aggressive offense from the opening tip, scoring the first 12 points of the game. Perhaps they'd been too aggressive, though, as they seemed to lose all steam. The Pistons went on a run and ended up rolling over the Lakers by 10. Dantley led the way for Detroit, combining for 52 points in the two matchups.

Detroit went to Los Angeles up three games to two, a game away from winning its first NBA title in the team's thirty-one-year history. In the third quarter of Game 6, Thomas raced downcourt and hit Dumars for a layup, but not before badly twisting his ankle. The Pistons' star player lay on the floor as Detroit fans around the country held their collective breath.

Thomas left the game briefly, but quickly returned, playing through his injury, and put on one of the great performances in NBA history. He scored 25 points in the third quarter alone, including 14 in a row, almost single-handedly keeping the Pistons in the game. He had to shoot the ball off of one leg, landing off balance to avoid putting pressure on his sore ankle. When he did accidentally put his full weight on it, he collapsed in pain only to get up and limp back down the court.

With ninety seconds left, Thomas hit a jumper from the corner to give the Pistons a 100–99 lead. They still held the lead in the final twenty-seven seconds, 102–101. Less than half a minute away from the championship.

On potentially their last possession of the season, the Lakers dished it to Kareem, setting him up for one of his trademark skyhook shots for the win. The shot went up . . . and missed. Yet the ref had blown his whistle! Laimbeer had made contact with Kareem, fouling him. Detroit fans couldn't believe it, yet they didn't need to. Laimbeer had fouled out, and Kareem went to the free-throw line. The steady veteran drained both free throws. Los Angeles 103, Detroit 102.

That would be how the game ended. The series was going to a deciding Game 7.

In Game 7, Thomas's injury caught up with him.

He played just twenty-eight minutes on the bad ankle and only made 4 of 12 shots. The Pistons shot 46 percent, while the Lakers broke the game open in the third quarter. James Worthy was brilliant, scoring 36 points, bringing down 16 rebounds and adding 10 assists—a triple-double in Game 7! Magic was his usual terrific self, scoring 19 points and leading both teams with 14 assists. The Pistons hung in the game, but Worthy, who would go on to be named MVP of the Finals, and the rest of the Lakers were simply too good. Final score: Lakers 108, Pistons 105.

The Lakers had done it. They had won back-to-back championships. They had won five championships in nine years. The decade had belonged to Magic and Bird, but on the court, the Lakers were clearly the best team in an era full of historically great squads.

The next year, the Lakers reached the Finals yet again, going for a third straight championship, something only the Celtics of the 1960s had done. They met the Pistons again, but this time, Detroit was too good, too hungry, and too determined to overcome another nemesis. Magic pulled his hamstring in Game 3. Abdul-Jabbar was 41. It was finally Detroit's turn. They swept the series in four games.

It would be Kareem Abdul-Jabbar's final season in the NBA. It was time for the next generation of stars and the next great team.

As if to prove that's exactly what the Pistons were, they began the '90s by reaching the Finals for a third straight year, beating Portland in five for their own back-to-back NBA championships.

THE FINALS OF THE 1980s
TOP TEN LIST

The starters get all the attention, but the sixth man—the first player off the bench—can be the difference between a winning team and a championship one. Here is a list of invaluable players who were just as important to their teams as anyone in the starting lineup.

1. Andrew Toney (Philadelphia 76ers): On a team of dangerous Philadelphia 76ers, he was the most deadly of them all, known for single-handedly taking control of a game and pouring on the points. Toney's scoring helped earn his team a championship in 1983.

2. Bobby Jones (Philadelphia 76ers): Fellow 76er Bobby Jones was a tenacious defender who won the NBA's first-ever Sixth Man Award in 1983,

the same year the 76ers won the championship.
The defensive specialist was named to the NBA
All-Defensive First Team eight times.

3. Kevin McHale (Boston Celtics): Started a Hall of
   Fame career coming off the bench for four years,
   playing behind Larry Bird. His illustrious career
   included three titles, seven All-Star Games, and
   two Sixth Man of the Year Awards.

4. Vinnie Johnson (Detroit Pistons): Known as "The
   Microwave," he came off the bench and scored
   points in a hurry for Detroit. He won back-to-
   back championships with the Bad Boy Piston
   teams late in his career.

5. Michael Cooper (Los Angeles Lakers): A defensive
   wizard who frustrated Larry Bird more than
   any other defender in the NBA. Cooper earned
   the NBA Defensive Player of the Year Award in
   1987—a year in which he won one of his five
   NBA Finals.

6. Dennis Rodman (Detroit Pistons): A colorful
   character with even more colorful hair (he was
   known to dye it different shades of blue, green,
   and red) who began his Hall of Fame career off
   the bench, proving over time to be one of the

greatest defenders and rebounders in the history of the league. Rodman averaged *13.1* rebounds in his career, which included two seasons of 18 plus rebounds per game, and was a member of the Bulls for five out of their six NBA Finals victories during the Jordan era.

7. Bill Walton (Boston Celtics): Resurrected his injury-plagued career with a new role in Boston, ultimately winning a title. Though his career was short, his list of accolades is long, including two NBA titles, a league MVP Award, a Finals MVP Award, and a Sixth Man of the Year Award.

8. Brian Winters (Milwaukee Bucks): An underrated sharpshooter who came off the bench for Milwaukee. Winters averaged 19 plus points per game three seasons in a row and was selected to two All-Star teams.

9. Roy Tarpley (Dallas Mavericks): A big man (he played both forward and center) who was headed for stardom until drug abuse got him banned from the league and ended his career. In his best season, he averaged a double-double—20.4 points and 11 rebounds per game.

10. Ricky Pierce (Milwaukee Bucks): Another Milwaukee sharpshooter who drove defenses crazy. His 23 points per game average in 1989–90 is an NBA record for a player who didn't start a single game all season.

THE
1990s

THE STORY
OF THE 1990s

~~~~~~

THE AGE OF JORDAN

By the end of the 1998 season, the NBA found itself in a place it hadn't really been before.

At the end of the 1960s, it was clear the Boston Celtics were basketball's best team by a long shot, but Wilt Chamberlain was the game's most dominant player. Meanwhile, the most culturally important sports figures in the country outside the world of basketball were boxer Muhammad Ali, baseball players Mickey Mantle and Willie Mays, and NFL quarterback Joe Namath.

In the 1970s, the field of talented players across the major sports was equally crowded. Kareem became the NBA's most dominant player. New York and Los

Angeles were the centers of the game. The legendary Celtics won two more titles, and Dr. J captured the imagination of kids across the country. Muhammad Ali remained a cultural icon, along with football player O. J. Simpson, baseball player Reggie Jackson, and teams like the New York Yankees and the Dallas Cowboys.

The '80s brought Bird and Magic, Dr. J and Moses, Michael Jordan, the Celtics, Sixers, Lakers, and Isiah and the Pistons. Lawrence Taylor and Joe Montana were dominant on the football field and redefining the arts of sacking quarterbacks and leading game-winning drives. Rickey Henderson was stealing bases like no one in baseball history and "Iron" Mike Tyson was a celebrity for his ability to knock out opponents with a single punch.

In those decades, there was a lot of love to go around, and no single player, team, or sport earned all the praise. All the important accolades had to be shared, across all American sports. In the 1990s, all of that changed. In the 1990s, one single per-son—Michael Jordan—stood above everyone and everything else.

He was the best, most dominant athlete in the

world. Tiger Woods would arrive late in the decade, but it wasn't even close.

His team, the Chicago Bulls, won the most championships. In fact, between 1990 and 1998, whenever Jordan was able to play a full season, the Bulls won the championship. Number 23, Air Jordan's number, became the most popular jersey number in the world. Yet Jordan's fame went well beyond the world of basketball.

From product endorsements and ever-present TV commercials for Nike to Gatorade to Hanes underwear, Jordan's image was everywhere. He even made a movie with Bugs Bunny. It's fair to say that Michael Jordan cast a shadow over American sports larger than any one individual since Babe Ruth!

Timing played a role, as it always does. The Lakers had gotten older. Kareem retired in 1989, and then the Lakers were beset by the devastating news of November 7, 1991, when Magic Johnson announced his retirement due to contracting HIV, the deadly virus that causes AIDS. The Celtics also had grown old and were no longer playing at a championship level. Debilitating injuries to his feet and back finished the hard-driving, nonstop Larry Bird. He retired following the 1992 season.

Only one of the established powerhouses of the 1980s remained: the Isiah Thomas–led Detroit Pistons.

And yet it was the Bad Boy Pistons that were perhaps most responsible for the transformation of Michael Jordan from great player to *THE* greatest player. During the fierce playoff battles of the late 1980s, the Pistons pounded Jordan. He drove through the lane and menacing center Bill Laimbeer would knock him to the floor. When he got up, Dennis Rodman knocked him back down. They challenged Jordan to be tough enough to get back up, stay up, and beat them.

When the Pistons dethroned the Celtics, Jordan and the Bulls became the next great threat. They had grown from a team that consistently lost games even as Jordan dazzled crowds with dunks and airborne artistry (like Julius Erving before him, Jordan once dunked from the foul line in an All-Star Game) to a team that was becoming playoff tough. They were surrounding Jordan with all the right pieces to succeed.

They were the first to hire Phil Jackson as coach.

They took a chance by drafting a lean two-way player in Scottie Pippen from little-known University of Central Arkansas; Pippen would go on to become one of the great defenders of the decade, making the NBA All-Defensive Team ten years in a row. Then they added the rest of the pieces to surround Jordan in a way that made everyone better. They drafted the tough power forward Horace Grant and then traded the tough power forward they already had, Charles Oakley, to the Knicks for a center, Bill Cartwright. They drafted young point guard B. J. Armstrong to pair with the veteran John Paxson.

Yet there was still the problem of the Detroit Pistons. Were the Bulls ready?

Getting through Detroit meant that the Bulls first had to beat all other challengers to the throne, primarily the Cleveland Cavaliers. The Bulls broke the hearts of a very good Cleveland team not once, but twice. The most memorable moment of those two playoff series came in a winner-take-all Game 5 in the first round of the 1989 playoffs: With just seconds left on the clock, Jordan hit the iconic winning shot that sent the message to the basketball world that he was not just a guy who could throw down amazing dunks, but was also someone who wanted to win as badly as anyone who ever played the game. Despite playing three All-Stars in their lineup, the Cavaliers never would get past the Bulls in the Jordan era.

The Bulls may have consistently broken Cleveland, but the Pistons continued to break the Bulls. In the 1988 Eastern Conference finals, Detroit destroyed the Bulls in five games. Jordan averaged 27.4 points in the series, but no one else on his team averaged even thirteen.

The next year, the Pistons beat the Bulls in six with the same formula: Let Jordan score his points, but beat him up physically and see what the rest of the team could do. Jordan averaged nearly 30 points over the six games, but the Pistons once again intimidated the rest of the Bulls, especially Pippen.

In 1990, the Bulls got closer than ever, only to lose again to the Pistons in seven games.

Three years, three losses in the Eastern Conference finals.

The hate between Detroit and Chicago was real; the rivalry between Isiah and Jordan held nothing of the mutual respect of Magic and Bird. Michael worked out all summer, lifted weights, and got stronger with one purpose in mind: to be able to take the punishment the Pistons would dish out in order to beat them.

The two teams met again in the 1991 playoffs, and the result would be very different. One team, Chicago, was rising. The other, Detroit and its two-time championship pedigree, was fading. The Bulls finally beat Detroit—destroyed them, really—in four straight, and the Pistons, true to their bad boy image, walked off the court before the game even ended. It was one of the worst displays of sportsmanship basketball had ever seen, proof of how much the Bulls and Pistons disliked one another.

It didn't matter, for the transformation of the 1990s was complete. In the 1991 Finals, the Bulls faced Magic Johnson and the Lakers. The Lakers won the first game, but Jordan and the Bulls rolled to win the next four for the first championship in Bulls history.

Now world champions, the Bulls looked unstoppable. Reaching the Finals again in 1992, they faced the Portland Trail Blazers. Portland provided a personal challenge to Jordan because the team had passed him over in the 1984 draft, and because the Blazers already had a high-flying superstar guard who played Jordan's position, the great Clyde Drexler. "Clyde the

Glide" was his nickname, and the high-flying Drexler was nearly as well known for his acrobatics and dunks as Michael. In the Finals, Jordan made sure the world knew who was boss. The Bulls beat Portland in six for their second title, but not before Michael nailed a record seven three-pointers in the clincher. Whether he was dunking over guys who towered over him, swiping away steals left and right, or draining threes, Jordan showed the world that he could do it all.

In the summer of 1992, during the Barcelona Olympics, something happened that had never occurred before: The US allowed NBA players to play in the Olympics. In the past, only amateurs could qualify to be American Olympians, but after a bitter loss in 1988 (the US had lost the gold medal in Olympic basketball just once before, controversially in 1972 to the Soviet Union), the rules changed.

NBA players were now eligible, and the US Men's Basketball Olympic team assembled one of the most dangerous, athletic groups of players the world had ever seen. The 1992 US Olympic basketball team called themselves the Dream Team—and they would prove to be the rest of the world's nightmare.

The rule change meant the great rivals of the

1980s could play on the same team: Magic, Bird, and Jordan. Drexler, Charles Barkley, and Patrick Ewing. One guy who was noticeably absent from the team was a young rising superstar center named Shaquille O'Neal, who was so powerful—standing at seven one and weighing 300 pounds—he reminded people of Wilt Chamberlain. The US team decided to choose one former college player selected in the 1992 NBA Draft, and despite the fact that Shaq had been taken with the first overall pick, the team decided to include Duke University's Christian Laettner instead.

O'Neal wasn't the greatest snub, though—that title went to Isiah Thomas. The hatred between Isiah and Jordan reached a head when Isiah was left off the most famous international basketball team in history. As the story goes, some people allege that Jordan told US team selection committee member Rod Thorn that he wouldn't play on the team if it meant he had to play alongside Thomas.

Yes, Jordan was so powerful that he could keep Isiah Thomas off of the Dream Team!

Basketball, by this point, had exploded as a world sport. Kids around the globe idolized Magic, Michael, and Larry. The Dream Team destroyed its opponents by an average of 44 points per game! Yet, because they were so famous around the world, even players from the *opposing teams* would ask their American destroyers for autographs. Jordan, of course, was at the center of it all.

The Dream Team rolled through every opponent, barely breaking a sweat. The Americans won the gold medal game by 32 points over Croatia. And Michael Jordan had now won an NCAA title, an NBA title, and Olympic gold twice (he had been part of the 1984 team while still in college).

Jordan returned the next season poised to keep his winning streak going. Next challenger up was another NBA superstar, Charles Barkley, and the Phoenix Suns. Barkley had begun his career with Philadelphia, teammates with Dr. J and Moses Malone. When Erving retired and Moses was traded away, the team sagged and Barkley was traded to Phoenix. He excelled with the Suns thanks to his tenacious will for rebounding, which was especially impressive because his build was slightly shorter and stockier than your average power forward. He was also an efficient scorer with a toolbox full of skills. Barkley could drive, dunk, post up, and hit mid-range shots.

Despite Jordan's dominance, it was Barkley who won the Most Valuable Player Award in 1993.

The Bulls and Suns met for the championship, and though the games were close, the Bulls never trailed in the series after three games. In Phoenix for Game 6, Chicago won the championship for the third consecutive year when John Paxson nailed the game-winner in the final seconds.

Nobody, it seemed, could beat Jordan. He now had three straight championships. He had no real rivals. His artful athleticism and grace made him perfect for the TV images beamed across the world. He had beaten Barkley and Drexler, wiped out the Pistons and also the New York Knicks in the East. The NBA had grown into the second-most popular league behind the NFL, but Jordan was by far the most popular athlete in the country.

He was also exhausted and struck by tragedy when his father, James Jordan, was shot and killed. Drained and in mourning, the great Michael Jordan retired from basketball. Instead, he decided to become a baseball player. He said his father had always wanted him to be a baseball player, and he decided he would try to honor his dad's wish.

For nearly two years, Jordan was gone from basketball, and without him, the Houston Rockets, led by the great center Hakeem Olajuwon, won two championships. The Bulls, without Jordan, were good, but the Knicks beat them in the 1994 Eastern Conference semifinals.

There were some phenomenal players and great teams holding down the NBA in Jordan's absence, but there was a void in the league so deep you could almost disappear in it.

Then at last, late in 1995, Jordan—hitting .181 in the minor leagues and with no chance to make the majors—returned to the sport that had made him king.

But Michael Jordan was rusty. Too rusty, and Shaquille O'Neal and Orlando beat the Bulls in the Eastern Conference semifinals that year and eventually reached the NBA Finals.

Jordan had returned, but could he get back on top? There was no doubt his game was still phenomenal, but he needed more surrounding pieces to help him get there.

The Bulls signed one of Jordan's great nemeses,

Dennis Rodman, the former Detroit Piston who had tormented Jordan and Pippen in the old days. Rodman was one of the hardest workers in the sport. But he couldn't shoot. He couldn't score. For all that he lacked offensively, Dennis Rodman was as dominant a rebounder and defender as anyone who had ever played the game.

With Jordan back, the Bulls ran through the league even more devastatingly than they had during the first Jordan era. The 1995–96 Bulls might be the greatest team of all time. (The 2015–16 Warriors might argue with that statement.) Basketball is a grueling game of endurance, with teams constantly travelling to games across the nation, but the Bulls left it all on the court every single game—and won almost every time. They won seventy-two games, at the time the most in NBA history, and lost just ten. Jordan won the MVP. The Bulls got their revenge on O'Neal and Orlando in the Eastern Conference finals, beating them by nearly 40 points in Game 1 and keeping that momentum to sweep the Magic four straight. They played another good but not great team in the Finals, the Seattle SuperSonics. Seattle was led by a defensive wizard, the guard Gary Payton, and power forward Shawn Kemp. The Bulls, untroubled, completed their quest and won their fourth championship.

They would win the next two championships over the same team, the Utah Jazz, beating two more stars of the decade, power forward Karl Malone and point guard John Stockton, the all-time leader in career assists. The Bulls-Jazz series were tight and competitive, but mainly served as a monument to Jordan and his illustrious career.

There was the legendary "flu game," in which Jordan played with a serious stomach virus and still scored 38 points. Then there was Game 6 of the 1998 Finals, in which the Bulls, older and exhausted by this point, looked as though this would be the time when defeat would finally touch them. Jordan, however, wouldn't let that happen. Down in the final seconds, he stole the ball from Malone, came downcourt and hit the final game-winning shot for championship number six.

So many greats before Michael had ended their careers a few years too late, waiting until their skills had gone downhill to call it quits. But Jordan had always been different and special. Why change now?

Jordan decided to go out on top and announced his retirement following the season.

When it was done, Jordan had won six championships in six tries (even Bill Russell, who reached the Finals twelve times, lost once). He was named Finals MVP in all six of the Bulls' wins. In all six Chicago championships, they never trailed in games after the third game of the series, proof of their utter dominance. No Jordan Finals series had ever gone seven games.

Jordan had faced every great player of the decade and toppled them all. In the East, he'd bowled over Ewing, O'Neal, and the long-range shooter Reggie Miller of Indiana. In the West, it was the same: Barkley, Drexler, Malone, and Payton all faced Jordan for a title and all lost. It took another sport entirely—baseball—for another team to claim an NBA title in the Jordan era.

There are countless names in sports whose dominant careers were remembered for years to come. Even fewer still are only a handful of players who have permanently seared their names in the history books of sports. Yet there is only one player who can be the face of a sport, the benchmark for every player who came before and after. If you ask any NBA fan who comes to mind when they think of basketball, there's one name that clearly stands above all others.

Michael "Air" Jordan.

THE STORY OF THE 1990s
TOP TEN LIST

Time is a cruel thing . . . so cruel that many of the excellent players and teams that played in the Jordan era have been largely forgotten by today's fans and are now destined to be forever known for nothing more than playing in his shadow. Here are the top ten teams and players that history would have treated differently had Michael not been around, or not been so incredibly skilled!

1. Cleveland Cavaliers, 1988–1994: Lost to the Bulls five times in the playoffs during the Jordan years.
2. New York Knicks, 1988–1996: Also lost to the Bulls five times in the playoffs during the Jordan era. They managed to beat the Bulls in 1994 in a seven-game series . . . when Michael took a hiatus from the NBA to play baseball.

3. Patrick Ewing: Speaking of the Knicks, New York center Ewing, one of the all-time greats to play the position, played in just one NBA Final in his entire career . . . when Michael was playing baseball. His team still lost.

4. Indiana Pacers, 1996–1998: Another very good team, led by three-point wizard Reggie Miller, that never managed to overcome Jordan.

5. Charles Barkley: Had a great chance to beat MJ in the 1993 Finals, but lost three games at home. The Hall of Famer never won a title.

6. Clyde Drexler: Without MJ, he would have been known as the heir to Dr. J. With Michael, no one talks about "Clyde the Glide" nearly as much.

7. Utah Jazz, 1997–98: Reached two NBA Finals, losing both against the Bulls. In both series, MJ was the difference.

8. Karl Malone: Won zero NBA titles in his twenty-year career in the league. Went head to head against MJ . . . bad idea.

9. Houston Rockets, 1994–95: One of only five teams in history to win back-to-back titles, but they're never mentioned as an all-time

great—because when they won, MJ was playing baseball.

10. Hakeem Olajuwon: Who was the best player on those great Rockets teams? Hakeem the Dream! He won two championships in 1994 and 1995, but Michael was (you guessed it!) playing baseball. Now the world will always be left wondering if he could have beaten MJ.

THE PLAYERS OF THE 1990s

~~~~~~

I n an era marked by the rise of Michael Jordan, an era in which seemingly every sports article or NBA broadcast was devoted to His Airness, it was as though the league was made up of Michael Jordan . . . and then everyone else. But in truth, that's a false view of history. Here are five other players who carved out a prominent place of their own in the age of Jordan.

HAKEEM OLAJUWON
Years: 1984–2002
Position: Center
Height: 7 ft.
Teams: Houston Rockets (1984–2001), Toronto
    Raptors (2001–2002)
Championships: 2 (1994, 1995 Rockets)

Most Valuable Player Awards: 1 (1994)

Jersey Number: 34

Nickname: The Dream

All-Star Games: 12

Hall of Fame: 2008

"Hakeem the Dream" arrived like something out of a movie: the soccer goalie from Lagos, Nigeria, who had really never played basketball until his height took the choice away from him. If Bill Russell at six foot nine was the first center to have the athleticism and jumping ability of a small forward, Olajuwon was the first seven-footer to have the same.

He played at the University of Houston, as part of the famed Phi Slama Jama team that also featured another future Hall of Famer, Clyde Drexler. In college, Olajuwon was known for blocking every shot in sight, wearing knee pads like a soccer player, and beating opposing centers downcourt for dunks with such frequency that even before entering the NBA Olajuwon had already changed it.

Following an assertive college career, Olajuwon was chosen by the Houston Rockets with the first pick of the 1984 NBA Draft (Michael Jordan went third that year). Within a few years in the league, he changed his name from "Akeem" to "Hakeem" to reflect its traditional spelling. Olajuwon would grow into one of the most polished low-post offensive players ever to play the game while maintaining a devastating defensive presence.

Olajuwon was one half of Houston's "Twin Towers" with his counterpart, seven-foot-four Ralph Sampson, and in Hakeem's second season, the Rockets dethroned the defending NBA champion Lakers in the Western Conference finals. Then they faced off against the Celtics in the Finals only to lose in six games.

Olajuwon was a master of moves. He had a turn-around jumper that floated up into the air and dropped cleanly through the basket. He mixed in a jump hook shot and the move that made him famous, the "Dream Shake," a body fake either inside or toward the base-line to move his defender out of position, after which Olajuwon could shoot or slide to the basket.

History will never know for sure if Olajuwon would've been able to defeat Jordan in the Finals, because Jordan went to play baseball following Chicago's 1993 championship. But there's no doubt the absence of number 23 created an opening for another team to step in. That would be Houston. In 1994, Olajuwon was named the league's Most Valuable Player, and the Rockets beat Patrick Ewing and the Knicks in seven games in the Finals. The following year, the Rockets swept Shaquille O'Neal's Magic for back-to-back titles. Olajuwon retired after the 2002 season, averaging 21.8 points, 11.1 rebounds, and 3.1 blocks, cementing his place as one of the last true centers to dominate an ever-changing NBA.

GARY PAYTON

Years: 1990–2007

Position: Guard

Height: 6 ft. 4 in.

Teams: Seattle SuperSonics (1990–2003), Milwaukee Bucks (2002–2003), Los Angeles Lakers (2003–2004), Boston Celtics (2004–2005), Miami Heat (2005–2007)

Championships: 1 (2006 Heat)

Most Valuable Player Awards: 0

Jersey Number: 2 (Seattle), 20 (Seattle, Milwaukee, Los Angeles, Boston, Miami)

Nickname: The Glove

All-Star Games: 9

Hall of Fame: 2013

The original big guard who could run an offense and play defense was Oscar Robertson in the 1960s. In the 1980s, another wave arrived in the form of Sidney Moncrief, Alvin Robertson, and Paul Pressey, but they were more defensive-minded. Magic Johnson was the biggest guard, at six-foot-nine, but Magic belonged to his own category. When Gary Payton joined the NBA in 1990 out of Oregon State University, standing at six foot four inches, he was a combination of all the big guards who had come before him.

Payton was a lockdown defender, who could stick to and frustrate opponents so much his nickname was "The Glove." Unlike Moncrief, Robertson, and Pressey, who were great defenders but not known for their shooting, Payton was a scorer, both on the fast break and from three-point range. Payton was also one of the biggest trash talkers ever. He came from Oakland, a tough basketball town where players talked as good a game as they played.

Payton led an athletic, sturdy Seattle team in 1996. The Sonics also had Shawn Kemp, one the most explosive power forwards in the game, Payton's back-court mate Nate McMillan, and a great cast of solid, unspectacular veterans like Sam Perkins and Detlef Schrempf. Seattle won an impressive sixty-four games and reached the NBA Finals for the first time since they won their only championship in 1979. But there was a big problem: They were playing the motivated Chicago Bulls, who had won a record seventy-two games and were hungry to get back on top now that Michael Jordan had played a full season. The Bulls won in six games.

Payton will forever be remembered as one of the greatest SuperSonics in history, but over time, the team declined and Payton wanted to win that elusive NBA championship. He joined the hated Lakers (Seattle never liked LA) in the hopes of winning a title, but the Lakers lost the 2004 championship to Detroit. He joined the hated Celtics the next year (the classic Lakers-Celtics rivalries had fostered bad blood between the two cities), but the Celtics were not championship ready. Finally, he joined the Miami

Heat, and after fifteen years of frustration watching other teams win the trophy, Payton finally got to hoist one of his own.

CHARLES BARKLEY

Years: 1984–2000

Position: Power forward

Height: 6 ft. 6 in.

Teams: Philadelphia 76ers (1984–1992), Phoenix Suns (1992–1996), Houston Rockets (1996–2000)

Championships: 0

Most Valuable Player Awards: 1 (1993)

Jersey Number: 34 (Philadelphia, Phoenix), 32 (Philadelphia), 4 (Houston)

Nickname: Sir Charles, the Round Mound of Rebound, the Chuckster

All-Star Games: 9

Hall of Fame: 2006

When he arrived in the NBA, nobody had ever seen a player like Charles Barkley. There were big, stocky guys who weren't that tall. Wes Unseld, the great Washington center, for instance, stood six foot six, 250 pounds. Unseld was big and burly, built like a tree trunk, and so was Barkley. The difference was Barkley was fast.

And strong.

And athletic.

Coming out of Auburn and selected fifth overall in the 1984 NBA Draft, Barkley was listed at six foot six, 252 pounds, but in reality he was closer to six foot four and a quarter, and he could handle the basketball like a guard, race coast-to-coast, and throw down serious dunks! Johnny Most, the legendary announcer for the Boston Celtics, used to call Barkley a "freight train" as he raced downcourt at full speed, over 250 pounds of mass coming straight toward you. And who was going to get in his way?

Barkley wasn't tall, but his base was so thick, he couldn't be moved. He had a tremendous sense of where the ball was going to land off the rim, which made him a fantastic rebounder, both offensively and defensively. He was wild, and the vision of Barkley racing, shirttails hanging out, about to jam on a bigger player, was one of the greatest sights in basketball.

Barkley was supposed to be another piece of a legendary puzzle. Philadelphia had the championship core of Julius Erving, Moses Malone, Andrew Toney, and Maurice Cheeks, but the team was getting older. Barkley was supposed to give them new life, and he did. But in a bad move, the 76ers management traded away Moses to Washington. Erving retired after the 1987 season, and Toney's foot injuries abruptly ended his career a year later. That left Barkley as a great player on a bad team.

He was revived in 1992, when Philly traded him to Phoenix, and a revived Barkley was a dangerous one. The Suns hadn't really been any good for fifteen years, but Barkley instantly made them a contender. Barkley was the star on a team with excellent players, like the point guard Kevin Johnson and power forward Dan Majerle. In his first season with the Suns, he was named NBA MVP and took Phoenix all the way to the Finals, where they played Michael Jordan and the Bulls.

Barkley was terrific, scoring 42 points in Game 2, but Phoenix lost both games at home. The Suns rebounded in Chicago, winning two of three on the road to bring the series back to Chicago, where the Bulls won the series in the final seconds of Game 6 on a three-pointer by John Paxson.

Barkley would move to Houston in 1996 and join an unfortunate list: the greatest players never to win an NBA championship. Barkley never held the ultimate trophy in his hands, but he was a Hall of Fame player who dazzled anyone who ever saw him play. When all was said and done, there was one list he added his name to that demonstrated how rare a talent he truly was—Barkley became just the fourth player ever to finish with 20,000 points, 10,000 rebounds, and 4,000 assists in his career.

KARL MALONE

Years: 1985–2004

Position: Power forward

Height: 6 ft. 9 in.

Teams: Utah Jazz (1985–2003), Los Angeles Lakers (2003–2004)

Championships: 0

Most Valuable Player Awards: 2 (1997, 1999)

Jersey Number: 32 (Utah), 11 (Los Angeles)

Nickname: The Mailman

All-Star Games: 14

Hall of Fame: 2010

Karl Malone was a six-foot-nine-inch, 250-pound scoring machine. He was a rugged power forward who defined the old-school meaning of the position. He rebounded, leading the league in defensive rebounds twice. For nine straight years, Malone averaged at least 10 rebounds per game. He was a prolific scorer who earned the nickname "The Mailman" because "he always delivered." For ten straight years he averaged at least 25 points per game. And unlike so many other great players, he almost always managed to stay healthy. Ten times in his career he reached the top five in games played in a season. For his career, he's second all time in minutes played. Malone was as reliable as they come.

He was an automatic scorer. Malone stood on the block, left side or right, and perfected his patented fadeaway jumper. Malone did not take wild shots or shoot outside of his range. He went to the place on the court where he knew he could score. In eleven of his first thirteen seasons, Malone shot better than 50 percent from the field, and no one got to the foul line more often than Malone. In five straight years, from 1988 to 1992, the Mailman led the NBA in free throws made and attempted, proof that he was always the muscle in the middle of the action. When he retired in 2004, Malone had made and attempted more free throws than any player in history.

Before Karl Malone, most basketball players looked either skinny or burly, but Malone looked like a weightlifter. Basketball coaches always told kids not to lift weights because being too muscular would make it difficult to shoot, but Malone proved that statement false. He played in an era of great low-post forwards, like James Worthy of the Lakers, Adrian Dantley of the Pistons, and Mark Aguirre of Dallas. There was also Kevin McHale in Boston and Charles Barkley in Phoenix, yet Malone was a perennial All-Star, playing in fourteen All-Star Games.

There was just one problem with the Mailman: Like Barkley, he spent his entire career chasing an NBA title and, like Barkley, never won. Like so many great players in the 1990s, Jordan was always his downfall. Malone reached the Finals twice with Utah, losing each time to Chicago. Malone reached the Finals again at the end of his career with the Lakers, but Los Angeles was wiped out by the Detroit Pistons. He scored more points than anyone in history except Kareem Abdul-Jabbar and finished his career arguably as the greatest power forward of all time, but winning a championship just was not meant to be.

Malone, along with point guard and assists master John Stockton, was the signature player in the history of the Jazz. The two made for one of the greatest duos in NBA history as an entire generation of Jazz fans grew up on the phrase "Stockton to Malone" for yet another basket for Utah.

REGGIE MILLER
Years: 1987–2005
Position: Shooting guard
Height: 6 ft. 7 in.
Team: Indiana Pacers
Championships: 0
Most Valuable Player Awards: 0
Jersey Number: 31
Nickname: Uncle Reg
All-Star Games: 5
Hall of Fame: 2012

Reggie Miller was skinny, like George Gervin skinny. He stood six seven, weighed only 185 pounds, but played with toughness and fearlessness. He was never the best player in the NBA. He never won a league MVP. He played in only five All-Star Games. He would never be in the category of Jordan and Bird and Magic, but for pure showmanship and taking advantage of a moment, Reggie Miller was a special player in the 1990s.

First, Miller was the star of the very good Indiana teams that were the first Pacers teams in the NBA since the ABA merger to be playoff contenders, perhaps even NBA championship contenders. Miller was the identity of the team, the guy who was always going to take the big shot and not be afraid doing it.

The NBA was late to adopt the three-point shot. When it finally did, in 1979, it was still not used as a weapon in the way it is today. Back then, it was employed as a shot teams would use when trying to get back into the game late in the second half. The first true NBA three-point practitioner was Seattle's "Downtown" Freddie Brown, but the first star player to provide a glimpse into what the NBA would become was Reggie Miller.

Miller was the long-range shooter before Steph Curry, Ray Allen, and Kevin Durant. Miller was the first player to make the three his primary weapon, and with that came a flair for the dramatic by being one of the great villains to opposing teams, taunting them both by jawing with their most famous fans sitting courtside and also by hitting huge, heartbreaking shots. Miller was the kind of player who made basketball fun: the guy you wanted your team to beat badly (but were also afraid of because he was so good!).

Take Game 1 of the 1995 Eastern Conference semifinals, Pacers versus Knicks, for much of Reggie's tale revolves around his constant thwarting of the Knicks. The Knicks had the game in the bag, up 105–99 with 16.4 seconds left. Miller took the inbounds pass and nailed a three, 105–102.

The Knicks scrambled on the next play. They couldn't get the ball inbounds. The point guard, Greg Anthony, fell down. Miller stole the inbounds pass, dribbled back to the three-point line and hit another from behind the arc! Tie game. Then the Knicks missed two free throws and a putback. Miller hit two more free throws, and Indiana somehow won the game.

When all was said and done, Miller had scored eight points in *nine* seconds.

Then he looked at Spike Lee, the famous movie director and die-hard Knicks fan, and put two hands around his own throat, his way of telling Lee his beloved Knicks had choked.

Miller hit huge shots against everyone, including Michael Jordan. The two even got into a fight once on court. But like the rest of the stars of the 1990s, Miller never beat Jordan in a playoff series, despite the big moments and clutch threes.

And like Charles Barkley and Karl Malone, Reggie Miller took his team to the NBA Finals in 2000 but did not win and had to settle for being another great player of the decade who made memories but never won a championship. It was a common theme of the decade for players not named Michael Jordan.

THE PLAYERS OF THE 1990s

TOP TEN LIST

ichael Jordan was the face of the NBA in the 1990s—and his legend is still at the forefront of every basketball fan's mind to this day. With great talent comes a worthy nickname—MJ was crowned "Air" Jordan for his otherworldly leaping abilities. Yet he wasn't the only player around with a colorful nickname— here are ten MORE of the best nicknames in NBA history (since there are too many to fit on one list!).

1. The Glove: Gary Payton, the Hall of Fame point guard who spent the majority of his career in Seattle, got his nickname from his cousin Glenn during the 1993 Western Conference finals series against Phoenix, when his cousin told him, "You're holding [Phoenix Suns guard] Kevin

Johnson like a baseball in a glove." Payton was a defensive wizard.

2. Clyde the Glide: Portland Trail Blazers guard Clyde Drexler was another player who impressed fans with his acrobatic dunks.

3. Hakeem the Dream: Houston Rockets center Hakeem Olajuwon received his nickname from his college coach who said Hakeem's effortless dunks "looked like a dream."

4. The Dunking Dutchman: Indiana Pacers center Rik Smits's Dutch heritage combined with his size (seven foot four inches) made his nickname a natural fit.

5. The Admiral: San Antonio Spurs center David Robinson's nickname has a very simple explanation: he was a Naval officer before he entered the NBA.

6. The Worm: Dennis Rodman, who played the majority of his career at forward for the Detroit Pistons, San Antonio Spurs, and Chicago Bulls, earned his nickname long before he stepped on an NBA court—his mother coined the name because he used to wriggle around while playing pinball as a child.

7. The Diesel: Shaquille O'Neal, the center who played most of his career with the Orlando Magic and Los Angeles Lakers, was known for his powerful play on the court . . . so powerful he was compared to a diesel engine.

8. Penny: Orlando Magic guard Anfernee Hardaway also earned his nickname during his childhood; his grandmother used to say he was "pretty as a penny."

9. Muggsy: Charlotte Hornets guard Tyrone Bogues, the shortest guy ever to play professional basketball (at five foot three inches), grew up playing on courts in his hometown of Baltimore, where his friends started calling him "Muggsy" after a character from the old show *The Bowery Boys*.

10. Spud: Atlanta Hawks and Sacramento Kings guard Anthony Webb was born during the Cold War, and his nickname has nothing to do with potatoes. His father's friend remarked on the day of his birth that Webb had "a big head like a Sputnik," a reference to the Soviet satellite of the same name. Webb's friends had trouble saying "Sputnik" so they shortened it to Spud.

THE FINALS
OF THE 1990s

~~~~~~

1994: HOUSTON ROCKETS
VS. NEW YORK KNICKS

I t doesn't happen very often, but sometimes, one play can define a career. It did in the case of Pat Riley, the coach of the New York Knicks. Before joining the Knicks, Riley had been the great coach of the famous "Showtime" Los Angeles Lakers of Magic Johnson, Kareem Abdul-Jabbar, and James Worthy. Though the Lakers would win three more championships after, Game 4 of the 1984 Finals against Boston would haunt Pat Riley for years to come. What looked like a sure Lakers championship suddenly turned into a seven-game series that would end with the Celtics winning.

When Kevin McHale took Kurt Rambis down with a hard foul, the play changed the series, and it changed Riley, who vowed never to have a team that could be pushed around again.

And so it was that when Riley left the Lakers in 1991 to become coach of the New York Knicks, a team playing in the Eastern Conference with the burly Boston Celtics and Detroit Pistons, Riley's teams would be tough and muscular, far different from the days when he coached Magic and Worthy fast-breaking for dunks.

The Knicks needed Riley. Despite being in the biggest market in the league, they hadn't reached the Finals since winning the championship in 1972–73. New York had Patrick Ewing, the star center and superstar collegiate player from Georgetown, who'd joined the team in 1985, but the Knicks could not overcome Boston and Detroit in the 1980s and now Michael Jordan and Chicago in the 1990s.

The Knicks lost to the Bulls in the playoffs in 1991, 1992, and 1993, but in 1994, Jordan had suddenly retired. While he was playing baseball, the Knicks overcame the Bulls in a seven-game Eastern Conference semifinal, then beat Indiana in another seven-gamer in the conference finals to reach the NBA Finals for the first time in twenty-one years.

The Knicks roster was made up of one star— Ewing—and a group of unspectacular tough guys, players like guard John Starks, who was a scrappy underdog player nobody wanted who found a home in New York under Riley. There was Anthony Mason, the burly, physical power forward who could pass like a guard. There was Charles Oakley, another tough guy who once played for the Bulls. In the middle was Ewing, who desperately wanted to live up to the expectations of his college days and bring New York a title.

Waiting for the Knicks was the Houston Rockets, a team that had won fifty-eight games that year. If the Knicks were full of rugged, physical players, the Rockets were full of clutch, explosive players with a legend in the middle. The Rockets possessed something very special and very dangerous: a roster of players who weren't superstars but excelled when playing under pressure. There was shooting guard Vernon "Mad Max" Maxwell, a streaky scorer who could take over games with his mid-range shooting, and forward Robert Horry, a reserve who seemed low-key, until the game was on the line. There was the point guard Kenny Smith, a native New Yorker who was so fast with the ball his nickname was "The Jet," and Sam Cassell, a fearless rookie guard out of Florida State. The legend in the middle was Hakeem Olajuwon, who had once taken the Rockets to the Finals in 1986, but had ultimately been defeated by the Celtics. Now he had a second chance.

The matchup also brought to mind the past: a rematch between Ewing and Olajuwon. The two had met in 1984 for the NCAA Men's Basketball Championship, and Ewing's Georgetown Hoyas had beaten Olajuwon's Houston Cougars. It was the first time the two titans would meet for a championship in the NBA.

Both teams could score, but at its heart, the 1994 Finals was a standoff between two great centers and two great defenses. Game 1 was a low-scoring contest, neither team even breaking 90 total points. It was a sign of things to come. Olajuwon just barely outplayed Ewing, and finished with a double-double, 28 points and 10 rebounds, to help his team edge out the Knicks at home, 85–78.

The Knicks won Game 2 in Houston in an

all-around effort. Olajuwon scored 25 points and Maxwell added 20 more, but the rest of the Houston offense was relatively quiet. The Knicks, on the other hand, had six players with double-digit point totals and New York managed to split their first road stretch, winning 91–83.

In New York, the Rockets won Game 3 when Cassell scored Houston's last 7 points for a 4-point win in New York. Houston's unremarkable 93 points in Game 3 would prove to be the highest team total for any game in the series. Three games in, three games decided in the final minutes of the game. It was a trend that would continue throughout the rest of the series.

Houston entered Game 4 with a chance to go up three games to one. Olajuwon put up another exceptional effort, continually posting up Ewing on his way to a 32-point effort. It wasn't enough. Ewing and Oakley were absolute monsters crashing the boards, pulling down 15 and 20 total rebounds respectively. The Knicks displayed another balanced offensive attack and pulled off a fourth quarter comeback. The series was tied at 2-2.

Patrick Ewing's ferocious rebounding was once

again a difference-maker in the next game, adding 12 more rebounds to his total for the series, but it was a former football player, O. J. Simpson, who *literally* stole the show during Game 5.

In an unprecedented move, NBC cut the live TV feed of Game 5 midway through because there was a major news story disrupting all programming, even the NBA Finals! Simpson had been accused of murdering his ex-wife, and while the game was going on, the American public was utterly engrossed in the police chase that ensued, Simpson trying to avoid the cops in a white Ford Bronco.

Meanwhile, NBA commissioner David Stern was screaming, "Don't do it! Don't do it!" as the NBC executives decided to shut off the live feed of the game and focus instead on the chase. Eventually, NBC showed the game and the chase together as a split screen. But only the fans watching in Madison Square Garden saw the full extent of the Knicks' victory in Game 5.

Suddenly, the Knicks led three games to two as the series went back to Houston. New York was on the cusp of a Finals victory for the first time in over twenty years. It was destiny, as the Rangers, New York City's hockey team, had just won the Stanley

Cup three days earlier, but the Knicks still had two major obstacles to overcome to match the Rangers' feat. First, they were playing crunch-time basketball on the road. The second obstacle was more imposing: Hakeem the Dream was determined to play his heart out and finally win a title.

The Rockets took Game 6 behind another amazing effort from Olajuwon. John Starks, for his part, had done all he could to help his team win, scoring 27 points in a heartbreaking 2-point loss. The Rockets' center thundered through Game 6, finishing with 30 points, 10 rebounds, and 4 blocks. One thing was clear: Houston's chances of winning the Finals rested solely on the hulking shoulders of Olajuwon.

It would come down to a winner-take-all Game 7.

New York fans would have the bitterest of memories. John Starks, the gritty kid who embodied New York and underdogs everywhere, had the bad luck to have the worst game of his career. After playing so well throughout the first six games, Starks made just 2 of 18 shots and went 0 for 11 from three-point land in the final matchup. In such a close game, just a couple of those shots might have made the difference.

Houston fans would remember the Rockets

winning the game 90–84 for their first championship in the city's history. They would remember Olajuwon's 25 points and 10 rebounds, and the rookie Cassell scoring 13 meaningful points.

History would always leave behind a great question: Would these Rockets have beaten Michael Jordan and the Bulls? Late the next year, Jordan returned but was rusty, and the Bulls lost to Orlando in the playoffs. The Magic, led by young Shaquille O'Neal, reached the Finals and played Houston. The Rockets destroyed Orlando in four games for back-to-back championships. Olajuwon solidified himself as an all-time great, one of the best centers to ever step on the court, and gave Houston a new nickname: "Clutch City."

1998: CHICAGO BULLS vs. UTAH JAZZ

When Michael Jordan returned to start the 1996 season, he did so with a vengeance. The Bulls broke the single-season record for wins with seventy-two, losing just ten games all season! They crushed Seattle in the Finals for their fourth championship. The next year, they won sixty-nine games, steamrolled through the playoffs and won the NBA title again, beating Utah. Jordan now had five championships and had been named the Finals MVP in all five.

Against Utah in the 1996–97 Finals, with the series tied 2-2, Jordan suffered a stomach virus before Game 5 and could barely get out of bed.

But he still played.

The Jazz saw Jordan was weak. They led by as many as 16 points. The Utah crowd was going wild. Jordan moved slowly, except when it was time to score, in an attempt to conserve energy. While Jordan nearly collapsed after every play, he played forty-four minutes and scored 38 points, including 4 points in a key stretch during the final minute that gave the Bulls the lead. He could barely stand when it was over, and his miracle performance would be forever known as the Flu Game. The next game in Chicago, the Bulls won the title.

By 1998, Jordan had already established himself as the greatest player of his time, which naturally sparked a new conversation: Was Jordan the greatest of *all time*? He was the most famous athlete in the world, but also the toughest. More important, he had enough gas left in the tank to finish making his case that he was the best ever.

And here, in 1998, Chicago and Utah met again for the title, the first Finals rematch since the Lakers and Pistons encore in 1989. The Jazz knew how close they had come the previous year. They still had the great duo of Karl Malone and John Stockton, who were hungry for their first NBA title. They knew they had let one slip away.

This year, Utah had home court advantage, and won Game 1 in overtime after Scottie Pippen missed what would've been a game-tying three-pointer. In Game 2, Malone struggled, and the Bulls took advantage. Chicago had a monstrous fourth quarter and that was enough to put them over the top and tie the series at a game apiece.

Back to Chicago. Michael's court.

It certainly felt that way during Game 3, in what turned out to be a disastrous moment in the series for the Jazz. Their offense was abysmal. Jordan scored 24 points, and the entire Jazz team managed just 54! The final lopsided score was 96–54, Bulls.

In Game 4, the Jazz recovered from their devastating loss in Game 3, and put up a good fight—but it wasn't enough. Michael Jordan and Scottie Pippen treated fans to an amazing display of offense. Jordan finished with 34 points, Pippen with 28, and the Bulls were suddenly up 3-1 with a chance to win it all in their final home game of the series.

But the Jazz weren't finished. Facing elimination in Chicago, Utah somehow came up with a great performance in Game 5. Malone seemingly single-handedly kept his team alive with 39 points as the Jazz won 83–81.

They were still alive, and they were going home. Two wins at home, and the Jazz would accomplish two things many people did not believe could happen.

1. They would win their first NBA title.
2. They would beat the great Jordan and Chicago in the Finals. No other team had.

The Bulls looked old. They looked tired. They were hurt. Scottie Pippen, Jordan's second-in-command, was playing with an injured back. They looked like many other championship teams had at the ends of historic runs. Utah wasn't much younger than Chicago, but they seemed fresher. There was talk in Chicago that, win or lose, Bulls management intended on breaking up the great dynasty in order to bring in younger players for the future. This was going to be the last hurrah.

Game 6 was played in Utah. The Jazz played with more energy than they had in the previous five games. Jordan was immense, trying to will his team to one more win and a sixth championship.

The Bulls had a rough start when Pippen reinjured his back after dunking the first basket of the game. He would finish with just 8 points. Jordan was relentless, though, keeping his team close, scoring 23 points in the first half alone. Despite Jordan's best efforts, the Jazz led by four at halftime.

The third quarter was basically a draw, and going into the fourth quarter, the Jazz led by five. Yet the Bulls weren't reigning champions for nothing. Jordan tied the game with a minute remaining.

But the great Stockton, at thirty-four years old, had never been so close to a championship. Filled with determination, he nailed a three-pointer with forty-two seconds left. 86–83, Utah.

Jordan, as ever, was unfazed. He raced right back

downcourt and scored a layup. But Utah had the ball and an 86–85 lead with under half a minute remaining.

Utah went inside to Malone, who held the ball and held the ball. He was looking to make a move when Jordan came from behind . . .

. . . and stole the ball from Malone! Sixteen seconds left.

Here comes Jordan. The clock is winding down. He's on the left side of the court, being guarded by Utah's Bryon Russell. Jordan shakes to his left, then darts right at the top of the circle, before cutting back to his left and rising up for the shot.

Ten seconds left. Jordan releases the ball, and twenty thousand Utah fans are rendered speechless.

The ball swishes through the hoop. Jordan is still frozen in his follow-through before turning back downcourt.

Chicago leads 87–86. Stockton goes for the game-winner to force a Game 7. It misses, and the Bulls are champions once again.

Jordan scored 45 points and was named Finals MVP for the sixth time in six appearances.

When it was over, Michael Jordan announced his retirement, and the Chicago dynasty ended. They would go down in history as one of the greatest teams ever, mentioned in the same category as the Boston Celtics and Los Angeles Lakers. The coach, Phil Jackson, earned a place among giants like Red Auerbach and Pat Riley.

At the end, just like at the beginning, Michael Jordan stood at the center of it all. When he finally hung up his jersey, he left the basketball world knowing they had witnessed the greatest player ever to grace the hardwood court.

THE FINALS
OF THE 1990s
TOP TEN LIST

There are too many sensational Michael Jordan performances to count, starting with his game-winning shot that beat Georgetown University in the 1982 NCAA title game when he was playing for the University of North Carolina. It's impossible to highlight them all—that would take a whole book's worth of top ten lists to do justice— but here are ten significant games in the professional career of Michael Jordan that separated him from the rest of the league.

1. The Flu Game . . . Game 5 of the NBA Finals against the Utah Jazz (June 11, 1997): MJ had the flu or food poisoning. He could barely stand up. It didn't matter. He scored 38 points in forty-four

minutes, and the Bulls won in Utah by 2. They went on to win title number five the next game.

2. The Celtics Game . . . Game 2 of the first round of the playoffs against the Boston Celtics (April 20, 1986): MJ scored a playoff-record 63 points against Boston. Michael Jordan had officially arrived.

3. The Shot . . . Game 5 of the first round of the playoffs against the Cleveland Cavaliers (May 7, 1989): Jordan scored 44, but the most memorable moment came when he hit an iconic game-winning pull-up jumper over Craig Ehlo to eliminate Cleveland. After that game, Jordan would be forever known as a feared clutch player.

4. The Final Shot . . . Game 6 of the NBA Finals against the Utah Jazz (June 14, 1998): MJ nailed the game-winning championship shot to win title number six. He retired following the game, going out on top.

5. The Comeback Game . . . MJ comes out of retirement (March 28, 1995): In just his fifth game after returning to the NBA, Jordan returned to Madison Square Garden and put up

55 points against the rival Knicks. His statement was clear: I am back.

6. The Career High (March 28, 1990): Jordan scored a career-high 69 points versus the Cleveland Cavaliers in a regular season game. As if that wasn't impressive enough, he also pulled down 18 rebounds!

7. The Shrug Game . . . Game 1 of the 1992 NBA Finals against the Portland Trail Blazers (June 3, 1992): MJ nailed 6 three-pointers in the first half of a 122–89 rout of the Blazers. After hitting his sixth three, he shrugged his shoulders in amazement. Even he couldn't believe it!

8. The Statement Game . . . Game 4 of the Eastern Conference finals against the New York Knicks (May 31, 1993): After going down 0-2 in the series and getting dunked on by John Starks in Game 2, MJ scored 54 against the Knicks in thirty-nine minutes to win the game and even the series 2-2. The Bulls won the next two games and eventually went on to win the title.

9. The Sweep Game . . . Game 4 of the Eastern Conference finals against the Orlando Magic

(May 27, 1996): After losing to the Magic in the playoffs the previous season, MJ got revenge this time around by scoring 45 points in forty-four minutes to sweep Orlando in the series.

10. The Giant Killer Game . . . Game 3 of the Eastern Conference finals against the Detroit Pistons (May 25, 1991): Jordan scored 33 points to give Chicago a 3-0 lead over hated Detroit. Chicago would finally beat Detroit the next game and go on a legendary championship run, winning three straight and six total in Jordan's career.

THE
2000s

THE STORY
OF THE 2000s

~~~~~~

A New Dynasty ◆ ◆ ◆
and the Return
of an Old One

For a lot of people, basketball as they knew it disappeared in the mid-1990s, and by the turn of the century, that disappearance was complete. Michael Jordan had walked off into the sunset of retirement . . . almost. In fact, Jordan ended up making a second comeback from 2001–03, this time with the Washington Wizards. But the experiment largely turned out to be a failure. Jordan still averaged a very respectable 22.9 and 20 points per game in those two seasons, but he never returned to his old form and the Wizards failed to make the play-offs in either season.

Finally, after Jordan departed for good, he left behind a changed league. Teams were no longer as important as individual players, a departure from the past when a team name was as important to players as it was to fans. In the 2000s, many of the iconic teams of the NBA—Philadelphia, Boston, New York, Detroit—all lost much of their appeal. Losing does that.

In earlier years, players needed a reason to enter the NBA directly out of high school—most commonly, their family needed the money—but starting in the 1990s, players were skipping college and going to the pros routinely without restrictions. Three of the most prominent—Kevin Garnett, Kobe Bryant, and later LeBron James—all were superstars in the 2000s. The result was an influx of players who were not only younger but less polished and less experienced compared to players who had played four years of college basketball to prepare themselves for the NBA.

The players themselves were different in other ways. The game had gotten so athletic that NBA teams now had only two true positions: the point guard (if they were really short) and the center (if they were really tall). Everybody else was interchangeable, capable of bringing the ball up court, even if they were six foot nine, like Chris Webber, the talented forward whose best years were with the Sacramento Kings. Most players now played multiple positions, and because the three-point shot had become an acceptable weapon, even centers and power forwards were so bold to take the farthest shot away from the basket. In the old days, the biggest guys stayed under the basket. Those days were over.

One thing, however, connected the old NBA with the new: the return of the Los Angeles Lakers as a powerhouse. The Lakers were down during the Jordan years, following the retirement of greats such as James Worthy, Michael Cooper, Kareem Abdul-Jabbar, and, of course, Magic Johnson, but one of the high school kids, Kobe Bryant, became everything the Lakers had hoped. He was the new Jordan, believe it or not. When Kobe took off into airspace, he displayed similar moves, similar athleticism, and similar electricity. As a kid, he had practiced so many of Jordan's moves they became his own. It was stunning how, in almost no time, the NBA had found a player who so resembled their best ever.

In addition to Kobe, the Lakers acquired two other superstars. One was Shaquille O'Neal, the mammoth center who'd played for the Orlando Magic. Shaq was the new Chamberlain, a giant at seven foot one and 340 pounds, who was just as unstoppable. He was the heir to the great Lakers center dynasty, from George Mikan in Minneapolis to Wilt to Kareem.

The final piece that rejuvenated the Lakers' dynasty was its coach. After Chicago dismantled the Jordan dynasty, Phil Jackson joined the Lakers. Like in Chicago, with Jordan and Pippen, Jackson now had two of the best players in the league, if not *the* two best, in Shaq and Kobe. The Lakers, having not won a championship since 1988, started 2000 a franchise reborn. The Showtime Lakers now gave way to the Lake Show and one of the great franchises was ready to resume.

The 2000s were going to be different, however, because something occurred that had never occurred in the game before: The Lakers had competition for dominance of the Western Conference. In the old days, the classic battles had taken place in the East, with great fights like the Celtics and 76ers in the 1960s, the Celtics and Knicks in the 1970s, Boston and Philly again in the 1980s, and Boston and Detroit at the end of the '80s.

The Lakers? Well, the Lakers always had control. When they were good, they beat up on everyone in the West. Not anymore.

For the twenty-three years they were in the NBA following the ABA-NBA merger in 1976, the San Antonio Spurs were known for two things: The first was George Gervin, and the second was never being quite good enough or rounded enough ever to challenge the Lakers. They had reached the conference finals in both leagues (having originally been part of the Eastern Conference) but had never found a way to the championship round.

Things began to change in 1987 when San Antonio drafted David Robinson, a seven-one center out of Navy. Robinson represented the new breed of NBA player whose height was the only thing that dictated his position. He was as quick as a forward with a reliable left-handed jump shot and, like Hakeem Olajuwon, had the speed to beat opponents down-court. Robinson was an excellent player, but a new era of Spurs' basketball really began a decade later, when they drafted power forward Tim Duncan out of Wake Forest and hired Gregg Popovich as head coach. These Spurs took off. In Duncan, the Spurs now had two big men who were fundamentally solid, terrific rebounders, and great low-post scorers.

Suddenly, the West had two titans. Robinson and Duncan in San Antonio versus Shaq and Kobe in Los Angeles.

In 1999, the two teams met in the Western Conference semifinals, and the Spurs swept the Lakers in four straight. San Antonio reached the Finals for the first time and became the first former ABA team to reach the NBA Finals, beating the Knicks in five games.

The next year, the Lakers won sixty-seven games and rolled to their first championship in twelve years, beating another former ABA team, Indiana. In 2001, the Lakers and Spurs met in the Western Conference finals and the Lakers got their revenge, sweeping the

Spurs, reaching the Finals and beating Philadelphia for their second title in a row.

The Lakers had won back-to-back championships. O'Neal had already solidified himself as the dominant big man of his time, and now he was a two-time champion. Bryant was proving that he was one of the great true talents in basketball and potentially on his way to being considered one of the best ever.

In 2002, the Lakers went for their third straight title. They met the Spurs in the semifinals again and beat them in five games. Kobe averaged 26.2 points in the series, Shaq 21.4. No one else on the Lakers averaged even 10 points a game, but two players, Derek Fisher and Robert Horry, proved to be two of the great clutch playoff shooters. In the Finals, the Lakers played a third ABA team, the Nets, and swept them for their third straight title. O'Neal was Finals MVP, averaging 36.3 points and 12.3 rebounds.

The Lakers had accomplished the rare feat of winning three straight titles, beating San Antonio in the playoff in the previous two years. San Antonio was hungry to respond to the Lakers. By the 2002–03 season, Robinson was thirty-seven years old, an old man by NBA standards, but two young players, guards Tony Parker and Manu Ginobili, stepped in and proved that they were not only very valuable players, but possibly also future stars. Ginobili was from Argentina, Parker from France, and both represented the new global popularity of the NBA after the Dream Team Olympics teams made basketball even more popular around the world.

In 2003, the Spurs got another chance at taking down LA, meeting the Lakers in the semifinals once more, but this time, the Spurs, younger and motivated, were ready. They split the first four games, and then the Spurs poured it on, winning the clinching Game 6 in Los Angeles by 28 points. They then beat an improving Dallas team in the Western Conference finals and reached the Finals, where they faced Jason Kidd and the Nets, who were making their second consecutive Finals appearance. Led by Duncan, who was the Finals MVP, San Antonio beat New Jersey in six games. Robinson, the great center who started the team's climb to respectability, retired after the season.

During the decade, the Spurs and Lakers overshadowed other good teams, like Sacramento and Dallas in the West, and New Jersey in the East, which had never been championship-level until the arrival of Kidd. The Lakers, though, were beginning to show signs of sagging and infighting. They added two former rivals, the great Utah power forward Karl Malone and the Seattle guard Gary Payton. The aging stars were still good enough to help their team win the West, but in the Finals, the Lakers were demolished in five games by the Detroit Pistons. Malone retired after nearly twenty NBA seasons, unable to win a title.

In the first half of the decade, either the Spurs or the Lakers reached the Finals every year out of the West, but the Lakers were no longer the Lakers. After the 2004 Finals, their legendary coach, Phil Jackson, quit, and then the Lakers' front office traded O'Neal to Miami in a controversial move. For years, Bryant and O'Neal's relationship had been fractured, and so the team finally decided to break up the duo. In the 2005 season, after the great trifecta had been broken up, Los Angeles didn't even make the playoffs. The Spurs, however, were even better than they'd been the previous season. Parker was turning into a star point guard, and Ginobili was all energy, all over the court, driving, slashing, nailing big three-pointers.

The Spurs met the Pistons in the 2005 Finals and won the championship in a classic seven-game series. The Spurs, who had never been to the Finals before Duncan, had now won three championships in seven years. Popovich had been the architect of all three victories. There was a new spectacular trio in town: Duncan, Ginobili, and Parker, who rivaled the great Celtics trio of Larry Bird, Kevin McHale, and Robert Parish.

After years being good but never great, the Spurs had arrived as a dominant force. The Lakers were back, but the 2000s were marked by the arrival of another phenomenon: LeBron James, who had been forecast for greatness since before he was a teenager. He was from Akron, Ohio, and was drafted by the hometown Cavaliers with the first pick in the 2003 draft. The year before he was drafted, Cleveland had won just *seventeen* games all season! A remarkable transition occurred over the next few years, with the remarkable James at the center of it all. Within four years, he had taken the Cavaliers somewhere they'd never imagined: the NBA Finals. They met, naturally, Duncan, Ginobili, Parker, and the Spurs, who swept them in four straight.

The decade was also marked by another return. After not reaching the NBA Finals for twenty-two years, the Boston Celtics—the team with the most NBA titles ever—were reborn. The Celtics pulled off an amazing trade, acquiring the great power forward–center Kevin Garnett from Minnesota and the sharpshooter Ray Allen from Seattle to accompany Paul Pierce, the Celtics mainstay. In the 2007–08 season, Boston won sixty-six games and met, once more, the Lakers in the Finals. Boston versus LA was an NBA dream, the league's two most famous, successful franchises going toe to toe. The Celtics, after two long decades, finally won championship number seventeen, beating Kobe and the Lakers in six games.

The 2000s were a glorious period for the NBA, with the resurgence of old staples and the rise of new giants. By the end of the decade, the Lakers had won four titles, and the Spurs had won three. In between, Shaq and Miami won the 2006 title. The Celtics were back. And though Kobe Bryant had begun the decade as the greatest player in the league, by the end of it, LeBron James was emerging as the most physically gifted player the league had ever seen.

THE STORY OF THE 2000s

TOP TEN LIST

From 2000 to 2010, with Shaq and Kobe at the helm, and then just Kobe when O'Neal was dealt to Miami, the Los Angeles Lakers won five titles, staking their claim as one of the greatest teams ever. The San Antonio Spurs, led by Tim Duncan, won three titles throughout the decade, securing their place in history. Those Lakers and Spurs are part of an elite club—some of its members were legendary dynasties, some were excellent teams, and some had the potential to win multiple championships but didn't win as much as expected. Here is a list of the best teams the NBA has ever seen.

1. Boston Celtics, 1957–1969: The Russell years. Eleven titles in thirteen years, including eight straight from 1959–1966.

2. Los Angeles Lakers, 1980–1989: Magic Johnson and Kareem Abdul-Jabbar's Showtime Lakers. They went to the Finals eight out of ten years and won five championships.

3. Chicago Bulls, 1990–1998: The Jordan years. They won three straight titles twice, first in 1991–1993 and again in 1996–1998.

4. Boston Celtics, 1980–1987: The Bird Era. They went to five NBA Finals and won three of them in eight years.

5. Los Angeles Lakers, 1999–2004: The Kobe-Shaq Lake Show years. They won three straight titles from 2000–2002.

6. San Antonio Spurs, 1997–2016: Duncan had been the centerpiece of a team that included David Robinson early on, and later acquired Manu Ginobili and Tony Parker. They won five NBA titles in six Finals appearances.

7. Miami Heat, 2010–2014: The LeBron Years. The Big Three (LeBron, Dwyane Wade, and Chris Bosh) won two NBA titles in four consecutive NBA Finals appearances.

8. Philadelphia 76ers, 1977–1983: Dr. J and friends. They made four Finals appearances in seven years and won one title.

9. New York Knicks, 1969–1973: The New York glory years. They won two NBA titles in three Finals appearances.

10. Los Angeles Lakers, 1962–1973: A team of Hall of Fame legends that included Baylor, West, and, later, Wilt. They went to eight NBA Finals and won one title.

THE PLAYERS
OF THE 2000s

~~~~~~

The Lakers and Spurs stole the show in the 2000s, winning seven out of the ten Finals of the decade. Kobe, Shaq, and Duncan were three of the giants of the league and shone on the biggest stage. But the 2000s were stacked with a host of talented players—here are five other superstars who mesmerized fans at the start of a new millennium.

LEBRON JAMES
Years: 2003–present
Position: Forward-guard
Height: 6 ft. 8 in.
Teams: Cleveland Cavaliers (2003–2010, 2014–present), Miami Heat (2010–2014)
Championships: 3 (2012, 2013 Heat; 2016 Cavaliers)

Most Valuable Player Awards: 4 (2009, 2010, 2012, 2013)
Jersey Number: 23 (Cleveland), 6 (Miami)
Nickname: King James
Hall of Fame: Still active

There was a kid from Akron who, from the time he was twelve years old, was forecast to be one of the greatest basketball players of all time. LeBron James was that kid. He was six foot eight, 245 pounds as a rookie, and from the day he stepped onto an NBA court, he would be the most physically gifted athlete the game had ever seen. Shaq and Chamberlain were bigger, but no player—not Jordan or Russell or Barkley—had ever possessed James's combination of speed, size, agility, power, and athleticism.

James was drafted right out of high school, and unlike other guys who'd come out of high school and needed time to develop their game, James was an immediate success, and Cleveland, a team known for losing, became instant contenders. In his rookie season, James blew away the competition, finishing with averages of 20.9 points, 5.5 rebounds, and 5.9

assists per game, easily winning the Rookie of the Year Award.

Too big to be covered by a guard, too fast for a forward, James was a power dunker who could also run as fast as anyone in the league on the break. Every matchup against him was a mismatch. He was a salesman for the game and for sneakers the way Michael Jordan had been, so his popularity with fans was immeasurable.

James was a one-man wrecking crew, and there's perhaps no better example of his dominance than his jaw-dropping performance in Game 5 of the 2007 Eastern Conference finals against Detroit. Cleveland defeated the Pistons 109–107 in double overtime, but here's what made it memorable: James scored 25 straight points and 29 of the Cavaliers' final 30 points. He couldn't be guarded, not individually and not by the whole Pistons team. He was the epitome of unstoppable.

James's presence created an immediate rivalry with Boston. The Celtics and Cavaliers played intense games as Boston returned to power and James became the signature player in the league. His battles with the

Celtics' Paul Pierce were genuinely combative. By the end of the decade, James had become arguably the most influential athlete in America.

He was outstanding in the 2000s and the Cavaliers were a powerhouse, but his best was yet to come, including three more league MVP Awards to add to his first in 2009, and three NBA titles, to name just a couple of his amazing accolades.

DIRK NOWITZKI

Years: 1998–present

Position: Forward-center

Height: 7 ft.

Team: Dallas Mavericks

Championships: 1 (2011 Mavericks)

Most Valuable Player Awards: 1 (2007)

Jersey Number: 41

Nicknames: The Dunking Deutschman, the German Wunderkind

Hall of Fame: Still active

The acceptable belief throughout the NBA was this: The tallest, greatest shooter in NBA history was

Larry Bird. Bird, a six-foot-nine power forward, had been a beast on the defensive boards and a fighter on the offensive glass who had also displayed impressive three-point range. How could a guy that big have three-point range?

When Dirk Nowitzki arrived from Germany in 1999, he had gone one step past Bird. Bird may still have been the better long-range shooter, but Nowitzki was something altogether entirely different. *He was seven feet tall!*

And so another change to the NBA became clear: There was a new class of tall players who possessed incredible shooting ability and athleticism. In the old days, just being seven feet guaranteed a life of playing under the basket. Not Dirk. Dirk Nowitzki was on the wing. He was on the break. He would stand behind the three-point line and wait for a pass. He could score from deep, but he could also post up (after all, he was seven feet).

Nowitzki represented the new breed of power forward. Karl Malone for years had been the standard, but even as Malone was a point machine, Nowitzki had greater range. He wasn't as strong a rebounder as

Malone but could play inside and was tougher than he was often perceived. Malone was great in transition, but Nowitzki might have been even better.

Like Malone in Utah, Nowitzki was the face of the Dallas Mavericks. The Mavericks reached their first NBA Finals in 2006, and it was Nowitzki who set the pace against the rival Spurs in the Western Conference semifinals. The Mavericks lost to Miami in six games but five years later would win the championship over Miami in James's first season on the Heat. Dirk had great teammates, like point guard Steve Nash (who would win consecutive MVP awards with Phoenix) and Jason Kidd, but Nowitzki would be the best player in Mavericks history and one of the standout players of the 2000s.

DWYANE WADE

Years: 2003–present

Position: Shooting guard

Height: 6 ft. 4 in.

Teams: Miami Heat (2003–2016), Chicago Bulls (2016–present)

Championships: 3 (2006, 2012, 2013 Heat)

Most Valuable Player Awards: 0

Jersey Number: 3 (Miami, Chicago)

Nicknames: D-Wade, Flash

Hall of Fame: Still active

When he arrived in Miami out of Marquette University in 2003, big things were expected of Dwyane Wade. He was a top guard from a school that had produced some good ones, like Doc Rivers in the 1980s, but within three years, Wade was already surpassing expectations and had won an NBA championship. He wasn't an automatic long-range threat like Reggie Miller, or a lock-down defensive guard like Gary Payton, or a high-flying rim-attacker like Kobe Bryant, but Wade was a fantastic combination of all of them. He had the size that made him difficult to guard, plus the power and athleticism to be a fantastic scorer. Wade was never a shooter as much as he was a scorer.

He attacked fearlessly, and when Miami made the deal to acquire Shaquille O'Neal in 2005, the basketball world assumed it would be Shaq who dominated the team. But in the 2006 Finals against Dallas, it was Wade who turned the series around with his defense and ability to drive to the hoop, as well as his mid-range pull-up jumpers. He wasn't afraid of the pressure that came with playing in the Finals. He wasn't afraid of losing, either—the Heat came back to win four straight after going down two games to none.

Wade, like Nowitzki in Dallas, was the longtime leader of Miami, but as the team aged and Shaq left during the twilight of his career, it was clear Wade couldn't do the impossible. He couldn't carry Miami all by himself, despite his tremendous gifts. After another losing season, Wade convinced Chris Bosh, the Toronto center, and the great LeBron James to join Miami. It was an incredible moment, for the front office had always decided which players the team would pursue and which they would not.

Wade showed the growing power of the players, who could now discuss with each other about where they would like to play. It showed a clear difference from the old days, where guys like Magic Johnson didn't *want* to be Larry Bird's teammate. If you wanted to be the best, the saying went, you had to beat the best. This generation was different. They didn't have to beat each other, when they could win together instead.

With the new trio, the Heat would become one of the great teams of all time. Wade found more spring in his legs. He had Bosh and James to share the offensive load, and the result was two more NBA titles.

KEVIN GARNETT

Years: 1995–2016

Position: Power forward

Height: 6 ft. 11 in.

Teams: Minnesota Timberwolves (1995–2007, 2015–2016), Boston Celtics (2007–2013), Brooklyn Nets (2013–2015)

Championships: 1 (2008 Celtics)

Most Valuable Player Awards: 1 (2004)

Jersey Number: 21 (Minnesota), 5 (Boston), 2 (Brooklyn)

Nicknames: KG, the Big Ticket

Hall of Fame: Not eligible yet

For years, Kevin Garnett stood tall in Minnesota, but there was no denying that he was following in the footsteps of other great players who'd found themselves in a similar, unfortunate situation—he was an outstanding player on a perennially bad team.

Because his team didn't win, Garnett was rarely on national television, even though he was one of the dominant forwards in the game. Like Kobe, Kevin Garnett made the jump directly from high school (Farragut Academy, in Chicago) to the NBA. He was raw offensively but a force defensively and on the defensive backboard. For a few years, the Wolves were playoff contenders, with stars like Latrell Sprewell and Stephon Marbury surrounding Garnett, but they were never quite championship level. It wasn't until the 2007 blockbuster trade between Minnesota and Boston that the course of Garnett's career was rerouted.

Now teamed with three-point sharpshooters Paul Pierce and Ray Allen, playing for the most successful franchise in NBA history, the Boston Celtics, Garnett soared. The country saw his game: the back-to-the-basket reverse-turn jumpers. The straightaway mid-range shots, the turnarounds from the baseline. He was a seven-footer with a smooth outside touch. Garnett really was, however, a fierce rebounder and defensive leader. Four years in a row, from 2004 to 2007 with Minnesota, Garnett lead the league in rebounds while putting up big-time points averages of

24.2, 22.2, 21.8, and 22.4 per game, winning the MVP Award in 2004. With Garnett, the Celtics' defense excelled, routinely making teams miss shots they'd usually sink. Garnett was an intimidator, the man in the middle the Celtics hadn't had since Robert Parish in the 1980s.

It was Garnett who restored Celtics pride and the team, once more, became a championship force in 2008, winning the Finals against Boston's eternal rivals, the Los Angeles Lakers. It was the combination of Garnett, Pierce, and Allen against LeBron James that made for a great Eastern Conference rivalry both with Cleveland and later on with the Miami Heat. The Celtics returned to the Finals in 2010, once again playing their ultimate foes, the Lakers, but Boston lost in a heated seven-game series.

Garnett also represented something else: in a game that had changed from a center-dominated sport to one highlighted by smaller, more athletic players (Michael Jordan, LeBron James), Garnett was a reminder that the man in the middle could still dominate a basketball game, and that while the straight-from-high-school route was not the best way for most young players, he was gifted enough to rise high above the pack.

ALLEN IVERSON

Years: 1996–2010

Position: Guard

Height: 6 ft.

Teams: Philadelphia 76ers (1996–2006, 2009–2010), Denver Nuggets (2006–2008), Detroit Pistons (2008–2009), Memphis Grizzlies (2009)

Championships: 0

Most Valuable Player Awards: 1 (2001)

Jersey Number: 3 (Philadelphia, Denver, Memphis), 1 (Detroit)

Nicknames: AI, the Answer

Hall of Fame: 2016

Like Elgin Baylor, Patrick Ewing, Reggie Miller, Charles Barkley, and Karl Malone, Allen Iverson never won an NBA title. He reached the NBA Finals just once, in 2001 with the 76ers, and faced the powerhouse Los Angeles Lakers, losing in five games. But greatness is defined by much more than the number of championship rings on your fingers.

When he entered the NBA in 1996, Iverson took a backseat to no one. He was the street kid who played street-kid tough night in, night out. A little guy with a lion's ferocity and determination. He was like the great Tiny Archibald, using his speed and phenomenal ballhandling skills to blow past his man and attack the basket with no regard for his own body. Iverson weighed just 165 pounds, yet for forty-eight minutes each game, he drove to the basket daring anyone in his way, whether they were six foot three or seven foot three, to try and stop him. He was the slightest guy on the court, and yet he never seemed to get tired. Seven times Iverson led the league in minutes played.

The uniqueness of his game was electric. Iverson was only six feet tall, and because of his height, he was considered a point guard, but Allen Iverson's true position was a scorer. He shot the ball. A lot. Iverson averaged more than 30 points a game four times and led the league in scoring four times. Iverson was one of the quickest players in the game with the quickest hands, leading the league in steals three times. Point guards are supposed to possess a pass-first mentality, but Iverson always played by his own rules. He led the league in shots attempted four times and was in the top five in that category ten times over a thirteen-year career.

Because he played so hard, because of his amazing point totals, and because Iverson was the kid from the tough streets of Virginia whose talents took him to the NBA, the fans loved him. He was a cult figure in Philadelphia, where he spent the first eight years of his career, including a miraculous MVP 2001 season, and took an overachieving Philly team on his shoulders and carried them to the NBA Finals for the first time since 1983. Iverson was traded to Denver, played in Detroit and then Memphis before returning to Philadelphia to end his career. His nickname was "The Answer," and for so many fans, that's exactly what he was—the answer to all their basketball prayers.

THE PLAYERS OF THE 2000s
TOP TEN LIST

The job of the point guard is to run the offense, get teammates involved, and distribute the ball to create offensive opportunities. Scoring isn't supposed to be high on the priority list for point guards, but some were so talented offensively that they could run the offense and also be a scoring threat at the same time. Here's a list of ten of the greatest scoring point guards ever.

1. Steph Curry (Golden State Warriors, 2009–present): Not only is he an unreal passer, but he may be the greatest shooter of all time.
2. Isiah Thomas (Detroit Pistons, 1981–1994): One of the first true point guards to be the primary scoring threat on his team and win the championship.

3. Jerry West (Los Angeles Lakers, 1960–1974): Mr. Clutch could score with anyone on the court. In fact, he was so good on offense, had he played in today's game, he might've been slotted as a shooting guard.

4. Chris Paul (New Orleans Hornets, 2005–2011; Los Angeles Clippers, 2011–present): CP3 can score inside or from behind the three-point arc, but he also makes his teammates better, finishing with double-digit averages in assists in five different seasons.

5. Allen Iverson (Philadelphia 76ers, 1996–2006; Denver Nuggets, 2006–2008; Detroit Pistons, 2008–2009; Memphis Grizzlies, 2009; Philadelphia 76ers, 2009–2010): A devastating offensive player and an incredible scorer who averaged over 30 points per game in five different seasons.

6. Gus Williams (Golden State Warriors, 1975–1977; Seattle SuperSonics, 1977–1984; Washington Bullets, 1984–1986; Atlanta Hawks, 1987): An explosive scorer who helped Seattle win the title in 1979, scoring 28.6 points per game in the Finals.

7. Nate "Tiny" Archibald (Cincinnati Royals/Kansas City–Omaha Kings/Kansas City Kings, 1970–1976; New York Nets, 1976–1977; Buffalo Braves, 1977–1978; Boston Celtics, 1978–1983; Milwaukee Bucks, 1983–1984): Once led the league in scoring AND assists with Kansas City, but later in his career he became more of a passer and won a championship with the Celtics in 1981.

8. Oscar Robertson (Cincinnati Royals, 1960–1970; Milwaukee Bucks, 1970–1974): Perhaps the greatest all-around player in NBA history. He defied the confines of having a position.

9. Magic Johnson (Los Angeles Lakers, 1979–1991, 1996): Not only was Magic a great scorer, but he was also as consistent as they come—he averaged at least 18 points per game in ten of his thirteen seasons.

10. Russell Westbrook (Oklahoma City Thunder, 2008–present): Another one of the current players who defies traditional positions, the high-flying, powerful Westbrook is a must-see basketball spectacle.

THE FINALS
OF THE 2000s

~~~~~~

2005: SAN ANTONIO SPURS
VS. DETROIT PISTONS

t first glance, the 2005 NBA Finals between San Antonio and Detroit was not a great series if you just looked at the box scores. The series went seven games but only one—an epic Game 5 decided by an epic game-winning shot—was decided by less than seven points. The first four games were blowouts by the home team, each game decided by at least 15 points, with the Pistons winning Game 4 by 30!

What made the 2005 Finals so great was the matchup; the champions of the previous two years were pitted against one another, the Pistons as defending champions, and the Spurs, who had beaten New Jersey in 2003, as the team fighting to regain its place on top.

The 2005 Pistons were special. They were an outlier—an exception—compared to the other championship teams that had come before. A common belief is that to win a championship in the NBA, a team has to have at least one no doubt, 100 percent, slam-dunk legendary Hall of Fame player, and a second player who is nearly as good. The Pistons had neither. Their best player was point guard Chauncey Billups, who was drafted by the Celtics and bounced around three teams before finding a home in Detroit. The next best player, Richard Hamilton, was a slight of build small guard who was a sharpshooter, but on his second team. Rasheed Wallace, the former Trail Blazer, was a power forward who could score and crashed the boards with intensity. He played with his heart on his sleeve, which sometimes meant he was a hothead on the court, picking up technical fouls at an alarming rate—so many, in fact, that he is the all-time leader in the category. At small forward was Tayshaun Prince, the third-year player who was a decent scorer and dedicated defender. The player having his best year was the center Ben Wallace, a guy who, prior to his time in Detroit, nobody, absolutely nobody, had wanted. Once, after being cut by the Celtics, a Boston executive told him to "find a game" and then come back.

But the Pistons were the rarest of things in the NBA: a collection of very good players with an amazing team bond who were good enough to win a championship without a player like LeBron James or Michael Jordan. They played *together*. They played hard, and every player on that team, while not a star, understood what was expected of them and made an impact.

Detroit won the championship the year before in five relatively easy games, beating the Lakers, a team that fit the common model of a championship team, as they were led by big-name players Shaq and Kobe. The next season proved to be an eventful one on the court for the Pistons, but not all the headlines were positive or even basketball related. On November 19, 2004, playing the Indiana Pacers at home at the Palace of Auburn Hills, the Pistons and Pacers got into a fight on the court that quickly escalated into a full-fledged, arena-wide brawl. "The Malice in the Palace" went down as perhaps the worst altercation in the history of the NBA, an embarrassing display where the Indiana players and Detroit fans fought in the stands.

Despite that ugly stain on their season, the Pistons won fifty-four games, beat the Pacers in a playoff rematch, and then defeated Miami to reach the Finals. Back in the Finals after their victory the year before, Detroit would attempt to be only the fourth team— Boston, Los Angeles, and Chicago were the other three—to win back-to-back championships twice.

Meanwhile, the Spurs were going for their third championship in six years. They won fifty-nine games, the most in the league, and had run through the Western Conference playoffs. The core trio of Tim Duncan, Manu Ginobili, and Tony Parker had already won a title together in 2003, then returned to the big dance the following season but lost to the Lakers. They were hungry to regain their title.

San Antonio entered the Finals having only lost four games in the postseason, and crushed the Pistons by 15 and 21 points in the first two games. Ginobili was the primary offensive factor in those two wins, scoring 26 and 27 points respectively in Games 1 and 2. It also didn't hurt that Duncan combined for 28 rebounds in the two contests.

The Pistons responded as only champions do, beating back the Spurs by 17 and 31 points in Games 3 and 4, every player on the team, starters and bench players alike, contributing in the two solid wins. Those victories set up a raucous Game 5 in Detroit.

Game 5 was a tight race from start to finish. The lead changed hands twelve times throughout the game, and the score was tied eighteen times. Neither team was able to mount a rally that would put the game out of reach. So with 3:10 left, after trading basket after basket, the game was tied at 79.

Both teams played rugged, tough basketball, from the guards to the middle. Though he was a guard and not a giant at six foot three, Billups's game was to muscle his way to the basket or find his way to an open three-pointer. On the other side, Ginobili was left-handed, and no one in the league attacked the left side of the basket as he could. Each side was filled with players who loved the clutch moment. Billups's nickname was "Mr. Big Shot" because of how many winning shots he had made. Robert Horry, who had already won two championships with Houston and three with the Lakers, also had a nickname: "Big Shot Bob."

Hamilton loved the moment. Ginobili loved the moment.

With 1:40 left, the game tied 85–85, Billups hit a fadeaway in the lane to give the Pistons the lead, 87–85.

Twenty-three seconds later, Horry nailed a three. Spurs up, 88–87, 1:17 left.

On the next Spurs' possession, Duncan was fouled, but he missed two *huge* free throws, which would've given San Antonio some breathing room. Still, the Spurs held on to an 88–87 lead with fifty-nine seconds left.

Fifty-one seconds left, crunch time for Detroit, and Billups made it count. He drove and scored, regaining the lead for his team. 89–88, Detroit.

With under forty seconds left, Duncan had a chance to redeem himself after missing consecutive free throws. Rasheed Wallace fouled him, and Duncan went to the line with an opportunity to give his team the lead. The first free throw went up . . . no good. The second free was good. Tie game, 89–89.

Then, with two seconds left, San Antonio had the

ball back with one last chance to score. Ginobili put up a shot, but Ben Wallace blocked it. Overtime.

In overtime, neither team could get a real advantage, but Billups pushed the Pistons closer with two more foul shots for a 93–89 lead with 2:51 left.

The lead stayed at four until Horry (remember that nickname) faked a three and threw down a left-handed dunk to cut it to two. Detroit led 95–93 with 9.4 seconds, when Billups missed a layup while being heavily defended by Duncan and Horry.

Spurs' ball, 9.4 seconds, down two. Horry inbounded to Ginobili in the corner. Rasheed Wallace left Horry open to double-team Ginobili, who kicked it back to Big Shot Bob, who wasn't going for the tie—this was the NBA Finals! Time to *bring it*. He was going for the win.

He nailed the game-winning three for a 96–95 overtime win.

That game had the feel of a finale, but the series wasn't over quite yet. Back in San Antonio for Game 6, the Spurs were one win away from the title. The tides had finally turned, blowout wins looking like a thing of the past, and it turned out to be a close one for much of the game. That was, until the fourth quarter started and Detroit jumped out to a large lead for the first time all game. They stayed in command, and the Spurs lost to Detroit, setting up a winner-take-all seventh game.

The Spurs were at their best when Ginobili and Duncan were in an offensive groove. Game 7 of the 2005 NBA Finals was one of those nights when Ginobili and Duncan were on point. They scored 23 and 25 points respectively, and the hero of Game 5, Robert Horry, added 15 more on the way to a Spurs victory, 81–74. San Antonio, which had never reached the Finals in the first twenty-three years since leaving the ABA, now had three titles in six years.

So many clutch shots for so many years made Horry a postseason legend. What was his secret?

"I just like to play the game of basketball," he said. "A lot of guys take the game so seriously. Even in pressure situations, I'm still smiling."

No doubt he was smiling when the Spurs hoisted their championship trophy.

2008: Los Angeles Lakers vs. Boston Celtics

The Celtics, a team that had once averaged a championship victory every five years, hadn't been to the Finals since 1987, when Larry Bird, Robert Parish, and Kevin McHale dominated the league. In the years that followed, the league had moved on from the old story of the Celtics being the center of the NBA. Sure, Boston still had the most championships at sixteen, but the Lakers were catching up quickly, boasting fourteen titles by 2008. The imagination of the game was now in different cities such as Phoenix, where Steve Nash had won back-to-back MVP awards, or Miami, where the cool D-Wade and Shaq played. Boston was old-school—and as the saying goes, out with the old and in with the new. The Celtics seemed like a thing of the past.

Rule changes that had taken place over the years had served to shake up rosters and spread talent across the league. Players could now control their own destinies and become free agents. Young, talented superstars wanted to play in glamorous, warm-weather cities like LA or Miami, not old, tough East Coast cities like Boston. The Celtics were yesterday's NBA. They had won just twenty-four games the year before.

But an old Celtics player, Danny Ainge, was now

the team's general manager, and he made a blockbuster trade for not one elite player, but two. Ainge
brought three-point ace Ray Allen over from Seattle
and the great Kevin Garnett from Minnesota before
the 2007–08 season. Allen and Garnett would team
with Paul Pierce, the Celtic who had toiled on bad
teams for many years, and the young, talented point
guard Rajon Rondo. Pierce, Garnett, and Allen had
all been All-Stars, but none had ever won a championship. Heck, none had even reached the Finals.
This veteran trio, plus Rondo, had one goal: to bring
a championship back to Boston.

They ran through the league, winning sixty-six
games. Garnett, having played for bad teams in a
city where the national TV cameras rarely came, was
now seen by the country as the great defensive leader
and rebounder he was, finally on center stage in a
major basketball market. The Celtics, down for twenty
years, were reborn.

They entered the playoffs as huge favorites but
struggled in the first two rounds, having to go seven
hard games with both Atlanta and Cleveland. In
Game 7 of the Eastern Conference semifinals at Boston
Garden, LeBron James and Paul Pierce engaged in an

offensive battle. James scored 45 points, and Pierce finished with 41, but the Celtics prevailed. The Celtics relaxed against Detroit in the Eastern Conference finals, winning in five games to get back to the title series, where an old foe awaited: the Los Angeles Lakers.

The Lakers were rebuilt themselves. Shaq was gone. Phil Jackson had left but had come back to coach again. The big question was for all of Bryant's brilliance, he had never won a title without Shaquille O'Neal—could he do it?

The Lakers won fifty-seven games that season. The great Kobe won the MVP, averaging 28.3 points per game. They lost only three games in the first three rounds of the postseason, sweeping the Nuggets, taking out the Jazz in six and destroying the defending champion Spurs in five. In addition to Kobe, Los Angeles had the versatile center Pau Gasol, the multi-talented power forward Lamar Odom, and the clutch shooter Derek Fisher.

Celtics-Lakers. The two most winningest franchises in NBA history. They hadn't played since 1987, when Magic Johnson beat Larry Bird in six games. Before the series it was Johnson who told Kobe, "Every great Laker has to beat the Celtics."

The first two games were bizarre: Pierce injured his leg and was taken away in a wheelchair in the opener, but came back to spark a big second half rally and a 98–88 win. The Celtics' core four—Allen, Garnett, Pierce, and Rondo—combined for 80 of the team's 98 points. In Game 2, the Celtics led by 24 points with less than eight minutes remaining in the fourth quarter, but Bryant led a ferocious charge and the Lakers went on a 31–9 run to cut Boston's lead to two with under a minute to play. But Los Angeles came up short in the end, and Boston won 108–102.

Fisher, one of the game's great clutch playoff shooters, left the court, vowing the series would not end in Los Angeles with a Celtics championship.

When the teams went to California, Bryant was superb, scoring 36 in an 87–81 win. Kobe was the key for the Lakers, and Pierce and Garnett the downfall for the Celtics. Pierce made just 2 out of 14 shots in the loss, and Allen was the only member of the great trio to score over 13 points.

Game 4 was the mirror of Game 2, with one

important difference: The team that came back from a huge deficit actually ended up sealing the victory. The Lakers destroyed the Celtics early on, jumping out to a 35–14 lead by the end of the first quarter, and then extending their lead to as much as 24 points. Unlike in Game 2 when the Lakers' furious comeback fell short, though, the Celtics put on one of the great displays in NBA history, going on a 21–3 run to end the third quarter, erasing the lead in the fourth, and coming all the way back for a 97–91 win to take a 3-1 series lead.

How could the Lakers bounce back after blowing a 24-point lead at home, now facing elimination? The Lakers trio of Bryant, Odom, and Gasol was the answer. Los Angeles won Game 5, roaring out to a 17-point lead after the first quarter and hanging on for a 103–98 win. It looked like the Lakers might repeat their Game 4 performance and blow yet another early lead, but they managed to hold on for the victory. As Fisher predicted, the storied rivals were going to back to Boston, the Celtics needing a win over the final two games to be champions, the Lakers needing to win both to pull off a comeback.

Game 6 in Boston. Bill Russell, the greatest

champion in the history of pro sports, was in attendance. The Celtics had waited twenty-two years to be
a game away from a championship again.

It was over quickly. Boston was too good. Pierce,
Allen, and Garnett, after all those losing years were
not about to let a chance to finally be champions
slip through their fingers. Garnett scored 26 points
with 14 rebounds. Allen scored 26, including seven
three-pointers. Pierce had 10 assists, and the Celtics
led by 23 at halftime, completely overwhelming the
Lakers. Phil Jackson told his team, "You're giving it
away. You're just giving it away." His pep talk did
no good. The Celtics poured it on more in the second
half, scoring 42 points in the fourth quarter alone,
and won 131–92.

The Celtics were back. They had engineered the
greatest turnaround in NBA history, going from 24
wins the previous year to 66 and an NBA title the
next. The Lakers would return to the Finals the next
year and redeem themselves, defeating the Magic in
five games. But 2008 was all about Boston. Finally,
the Celtics had restored their reputation as the NBA's
best franchise.

THE FINALS OF THE 2000s

TOP TEN LIST

n professional sports, it all comes down to the championship. Every minute of every game is played with one goal in mind—earning the honor of being the best team in the league at season's end. History has shown that the greatest players rise to the occasion when it's all on the line, saving their best basketball for the Finals. The top individual performers—the difference-makers, the X-factors—are ultimately rewarded with the NBA Finals Most Valuable Player Award. Here are ten of the most memorable MVP performances in the history of the NBA Finals.

1. Jerry West, Los Angeles Lakers (1969): The only member of a losing team ever to win the Finals

MVP Award. He averaged an impressive 37.9 points per game in the loss to the Celtics.

2. Michael Jordan, Chicago Bulls (1997): No victory is ever single-handed, but he was the difference against Utah. His 32.3 points, 7 rebounds, and 6 assists per game are just a glimpse at how great he was throughout the series.

3. Kareem Abdul-Jabbar, Los Angeles Lakers (1985): Tired of losing to the Celtics, Kareem said enough was enough. His dominant performance included near double-double averages (25.7 points and 9 rebounds per game).

4. Larry Bird, Boston Celtics (1986): Nearly averaged a triple-double (24 points, 9.7 rebounds, 9.5 assists) in a six-game series against the Rockets.

5. Magic Johnson, Los Angeles Lakers (1987): Hit the signature, game-winning hook shot of the series in Game 4 in Boston, and finished with averages of 26.2 points, 8 rebounds, and 13 assists per game.

6. Wilt Chamberlain, Los Angeles Lakers (1972): He averaged 19.4 points and 23.2 rebounds per game against the Knicks . . . at age thirty-five.

7. Moses Malone, Philadelphia 76ers (1983): He was the catalyst for Philadelphia against Los Angeles and the main reason the 76ers finally got the chance to hold the championship trophy. When it was over, the box score read 25.8 points and 18 rebounds per game in the series.

8. LeBron James, Miami Heat (2012): James's first title came with a powerful performance against Oklahoma City—28.6 points, 10.2 rebounds, and 7.4 assists per game. The Heat needed just five games to win the title.

9. Dwyane Wade, Miami Heat (2006): Averaged 34.7 points in Miami's six-game win over Dallas.

10. Dennis Johnson, Seattle SuperSonics (1979): The defensive specialist came up big offensively against the Washington Bullets, averaging 22.6 points, 6 rebounds, and 6 assists per game from the guard position.

THE
2010s

THE STORY
OF THE 2010s

Of a King and Change

I n 2010, the twenty-first century entered its tenth
year, and just when it seemed like basketball
couldn't evolve any more, it did. The basketball
world had already witnessed the physical evolution of its players, who were now bigger, faster, and
stronger than players of past eras. The NBA had also
witnessed the cultural evolution of basketball, which
had developed into an international game. Raised
on the Dream Team, a great number of players were
now coming from Europe (Dirk Nowitzki, Tony
Parker), South America (Manu Ginobili), China (Yao
Ming), and even Australia (Andrew Bogut) to play in
the NBA.

But the 2010s opened up two new areas that basketball hadn't seen before. The first was the power of the player. Players had already been offered rich contracts for years, but now they were communicating in a way they never had before when it came to free agency. In the past, when a player's contract was up and he was free to switch teams, an organization's front office might reach out to that player if they wanted to sign him. Now players who had been familiar with one another since they were younger on traveling teams, or had played together in All-Star Games and Olympic competition, or trained together in the off-season, cut out the front office middlemen and reached out to each other directly, hoping to recruit new teammates.

The old guard of players was furious. This wasn't competition. Why would great players team up instead of wanting to beat each other? Had Wilt and Russell wanted to be teammates? Magic and Larry? Or Michael and Charles? Of course not!

The saying went like this: if you want to be the best, you have to beat the best.

But today's players saw things differently.

It all came to a head surrounding the game's

greatest player, LeBron James. James had single-handedly changed the history of Cleveland basketball. The Cavaliers, once losers, were now a top team whose games were played on national TV all the time. They also won all the time. In 2007, James's third season, he took the Cavaliers to the NBA Finals. They were swept by San Antonio, but James had made people in Cleveland think big. Over the next three years, Cleveland was something they had never been before: A prime contender four straight years.

When James was eligible to become a free agent after the 2010 season, he and Miami star Dwyane Wade and Toronto star Chris Bosh (also a free agent) agreed to join forces and create a super-team. In an unprecedented television special called "The Decision," created to announce the team James had chosen, James declared, "I've decided to take my talents to South Beach."

James left Cleveland and joined Bosh and Wade in Miami.

Fans in Cleveland went crazy. They called him a traitor. Some even lit his jersey on fire. Dan Gilbert, the owner, wrote a letter saying Cleveland was better off without James, the best player in the world.

But he was gone, and the result was indeed a super-team. The Heat were suddenly the favorites to win. James was by far the best player in basketball, and night in and night out, he proved it.

Cleveland felt it, too. Gilbert couldn't have been more wrong. Without James, Cleveland went from 61 wins in 2009–10 to 19 wins the following season. Meanwhile, the Heat reached the NBA Finals, where they played nervous, unconfident basketball and lost in a six-game stunner to the Dallas Mavericks.

The NBA belonged almost solely to James. There was a galaxy of new stars: Chris Paul of the Clippers, Paul George of the Pacers, Carmelo Anthony in New York, Kevin Durant, James Harden, and Russell Westbrook in Oklahoma City. Yet none were quite able to challenge James. He was bigger, faster, and stronger than his peers. He was unstoppable when he needed to score, barreling his six-foot-eight, 250-pound frame to the basket. With Wade and Bosh alongside him, no team had as good a combination of stars. Even the Pierce-Allen-Garnett Celtics had gotten old. The league was set up for a James dynasty.

The next year, James and his teammates had to wait a little longer than usual to step back on the court. The collective bargaining agreement, a contract between the NBA—meaning the league office and the team owners—and the Players Association, which determined the rules for player contracts, trades, and much more, expired and the two sides struggled to come to a new agreement. Eventually they came to a mutual understanding, but not before the season was cut short by sixteen games.

When order was restored, James was even better than he'd been the previous year, and the Heat mowed down the NBA for a second year, finishing the regular season with a record of 46-20. They even destroyed James's bitter rivals, the Celtics, who were vying for an upset in the Eastern Conference finals, only to have James score 45 points in Game 6 in Boston. The Heat won easily in Game 7 and went to the Finals for the second straight year.

They faced the young superstar and prolific scorer Kevin Durant of Oklahoma City in the Finals. James and Durant were considered the two best players in the game and had a chance to become the Magic and Bird of a new era. Durant and the Thunder won the first game of the Series. But that was as close as they would come to a championship. James and the Heat took control of the series, winning four straight and an NBA title—James's first.

James would take the Heat to the Finals the next two years, playing against the Spurs in both series. The first was a classic seven-game series, won eventually by Miami, even though in an epic Game 6, San Antonio had been twenty seconds away from winning the championship.

The next year, the Spurs sought revenge all season and got it, meeting James and Miami again, this time taking care of business in five quick games.

Yet James wasn't done turning the basketball world upside down. After going to four straight Finals, and winning two of them, he decided it was once again time to shake up the state of the NBA. The summer after the Spurs' victory in the Finals, James chose to return to Cleveland, going back to the city where he'd discovered his love of the game and the basketball world had discovered his incredible skills. He was joined by Kevin Love, the talented rebounder and scorer formerly of the Minnesota Timberwolves, and the promising young guard Kyrie Irving, who'd been selected number one overall in the 2011 NBA Draft.

The balance shifted as LeBron shifted, and Cleveland was suddenly championship material. Yes, LeBron James was so good that whatever team he played for was an automatic favorite to win the title.

The second change in the NBA during the 2010s was the debunking of the old notion that winning a championship could not be done from outside the three-point arc. The thinking for the past fifty years had been that the closer the game was played to the basket, the better the chance your team had of going all the way. Jump-shooting teams just didn't win the championship.

And then the Golden State Warriors came along.

It all started with Steph Curry, a thin, sharpshooting guard drafted in 2009 by the Warriors in the first round. Curry was the son of Dell Curry, one of the great long-range shooters in the 1980s and 1990s. Steph was a first-rounder, picked seventh, after a surprisingly successful college career at the small liberal arts college of Davidson. However, his small frame caused many coaches to pass on him, questioning how well his skill set would serve him in the NBA.

What no one but perhaps the Warriors saw was that Curry was a can't-miss, special player. The

Warriors began building a team around him that was unlike any team ever constructed in the NBA, with shooters of all sizes at every position. They could run and shoot and defend, and played with a championship-level toughness that was easy to underestimate. Curry possessed all the skills of the greats of the past but also the championship desire reserved for the very best.

Maybe the Warriors signified a new way of playing. Maybe the Warriors had reinvented the modern game. It was a three-point shooting game now, and unlike other teams, the Warriors created a roster to reflect that speed, versatility, and outside shooting were more important than constructing a team based on the traditionally prized skill sets of the five positions. Today, NBA teams shoot more three-pointers than ever before, but the Warriors shot the three better than the rest, and Curry the best of them all (though teammate Klay Thompson, the other half of the "Splash Brothers" duo, wasn't too far behind). Still, when the 2015 playoffs rolled around, their freewheeling, free-shooting, undersized ways would abandon them, right? Surely a team built upon the three ball couldn't win it all?

Wrong.

Even if their opponent in the NBA Finals was none other than LeBron James, now in Cleveland, making his fifth straight appearance in the Finals, something not even Michael Jordan ever did! Only Bill Russell and the Celtics had ever appeared in five straight, and that was back in the 1960s.

When Cleveland, with stars Kyrie Irving and Kevin Love both injured, took a 2-1 lead with only James and the unsung backup Matthew Dellavedova playing well, it appeared the Warriors' freewheeling ways were being exposed.

Then the Warriors won three straight and the championship. Convincingly. James looked worn out, even a little old.

Even after their victory, many critics were eager to declare the 2015 Warriors a fluke. The Warriors returned the next season, upset that critics said they didn't deserve their title, and were even more dominant, starting the season 24-0. Then they played James and the Cavaliers twice in the span of a month and beat them at home in the first, close game, and embarrassed them in Cleveland in the second, easily winning by 34 points. As the decade reached its halfway point, one thing was clear: Curry was the reigning league MVP, poised to win another, and suddenly, LeBron James wasn't the only game in town anymore.

The Warriors were only getting started. They were the champions. They had won 24 in a row. They had beaten James twice after beating him in the Finals. Now, they had their eyes on another, bigger target: Michael Jordan and the 1995–96, 72-win, greatest season of all time Chicago Bulls.

They played every game with purpose, even in the long, backbreaking NBA season. They went after every loose ball, every record. They were unbeaten at home, hoping to become the only team in NBA history to go 41-0 at home. The Celtics went 40-1 in 1985–86, and it was the Celtics who beat them to prevent that streak.

Nothing prevented them from passing the Bulls, however, as Golden State won seventy-three games!

Then, Steph Curry, to the frustration of James, was named MVP a second straight year, but this time unanimously, a feat that no player, not Magic or Bird, Wilt or Russell, Jordan or James, had ever accomplished. All that was left was the hardest feat:

winning the 2016 championship. Curry was a defending champion, now a two-time MVP. His team had
won more games than any other in NBA history. The
center of the NBA seemed to be moving from James
in Cleveland to Curry in Oakland, but LeBron James
would have something to say about the idea of Steph
Curry taking over the league.

THE STORY OF THE 2010s
TOP TEN LIST

Steph Curry is rewriting the record books as the game of basketball continues to change, with teams now relying more heavily on three-point shooting. But the NBA has always had a host of incredible sharpshooters, long before this era of video-game-caliber shooting. Here are some of the very best.

1. Larry Bird (Boston Celtics, 1979–1992): A three-time Three-Point Contest champ. He had unlimited range, especially for a guy who was six foot nine.

2. Steph Curry (Golden State Warriors, 2009– present): Not just a shooter but a scorer from anywhere on the court. He makes the kind of shots in an NBA game that kids chuck up in

their driveways, dreaming of hitting a half-court buzzer beater . . . something Steph has done on multiple occasions! He's that good.

3. Kareem Abdul-Jabbar (Milwaukee Bucks, 1969–1975; Los Angeles Lakers, 1975–1989): Had the most unstoppable shot in NBA history: the skyhook.

4. Reggie Miller (Indiana Pacers, 1987–2005): Had long-distance range, midrange, and one other thing: the clutch factor! He could reliably hit a three with the game on the line.

5. Ray Allen (Milwaukee Bucks, 1996–2003; Seattle SuperSonics, 2003–2007; Boston Celtics, 2007–2012; Miami Heat, 2012–2014): Holds the all-time record for three-pointers, but Curry will break it at some point.

6. Jerry West (Los Angeles Lakers, 1960–1974): A high-volume shooter in an era when few players could make a basket.

7. Dirk Nowitzki (Dallas Mavericks, 1994–present): Replaced Larry Bird as the tallest, best shooter ever. A seven-footer with three-point range.

8. Kevin Durant (Oklahoma City Thunder, 2007–2016, Golden State Warriors 2016–present): At

six foot nine inches, he's another player in the tradition of tall players with three-point shooting range.

9. John Stockton (Utah Jazz, 1984–2003): Though he wasn't known as a three-point shooter, Stockton was reliable from behind the arc, and his mid-range shooting was even more efficient. He finished his career with a 51.5 shooting percentage.

10. Klay Thompson (Golden State Warriors, 2011– present): The other half of the best-shooting backcourt in NBA history.

THE PLAYERS OF THE 2010s

~~~~~~

The 2010s isn't even finished yet, but we've already witnessed the continued greatness of LeBron James and the arrival of new superstars like Steph Curry, Kevin Durant, and Russell Westbrook. Who knows how many more phenoms will take center stage before the decade is over? But for now, here are the players who have owned the 2010s so far.

STEPHEN CURRY

Years: 2009–present

Position: Point guard

Height: 6 ft. 3 in.

Team: Golden State Warriors

Championships: 1 (2015 Warriors)

Most Valuable Player Awards: 2 (2015, 2016)

Jersey Number: 30

Nicknames: Chef, Baby-Faced Assassin

Hall of Fame: Still active

If the Golden State Warriors knew Steph Curry was going to be the can't-miss superstar he turned out to be when they drafted him seventh in the 2009 draft, they were probably the only ones. Not that people didn't think he was good. Curry was the son of long-range NBA marksman Dell Curry, so he had been steeped in the game since birth.

But by his fourth year, Curry could shoot like Bird, dribble like Isiah, pass like Magic, and show off the creative scoring flair of Gervin and Pete Maravich, making shots most kids only tried *after* practice. Oh, and one other thing: Curry possessed the ruthless drive of Michael Jordan to be great and win.

By 2014, Curry had established himself as a giant of the league, and the Warriors had proven they were a top-tier team. That year, the Warriors went deep in the playoffs but were ultimately thwarted by Tim Duncan and the Spurs, losing in a six-game Western Conference finals. Then in 2015, led by Curry, Golden State ran through the league with a dazzling array of passing, shooting, teamwork, and toughness, finishing off their banner year with a shocking championship win against James and the Cavs.

Curry has all the moves, all the shots, all the range. His scoring instincts have made him one of the most exciting players to watch. It isn't that Steph can shoot just threes, which he does better than anyone else in the league, but also runners and scoop shots and bank shots and finger rolls. He's the total offense package.

Maybe if left alone, without the kind of talent around him, Curry would be easier to stop. But the Warriors became champions by putting Curry in the middle of an offensive machine, with backcourt mate Klay Thompson, do-everything forward Draymond Green, forward Harrison Barnes, and dependable sixth man Andre Iguodala.

Don't let the smile and baby face fool you—Steph Curry is downright dangerous on the court. Need proof? Look no further than the results of the 2015 NBA MVP voting—Curry won, beating out the King himself, LeBron James, and also won a title to cap off a momentous season.

Even though the next season would end with a stunning upset loss in an NBA Finals rematch against the great LeBron James, the Warriors won seventy-three games and Curry was named the only unanimous MVP in league history. Each season from 2012–13 to 2015–16 (and likely beyond), he took and made more three-pointers than anyone in the league. As proof of how much his great shooting has changed the way the game is played, Curry made 402 threes in 2015–16, just 247 fewer than the great Larry Bird made in his entire thirteen-year career!

Curry's will to win is the difference-maker, and the rest of the NBA is finding out the hard way.

CHRIS PAUL

Years: 2005–present

Position: Point guard

Height: 6 ft.

Teams: New Orleans/Oklahoma City Hornets (2005–2007), New Orleans Hornets (2007–2011), Los Angeles Clippers (2011–present)

Championships: 0

Most Valuable Player Awards: 0

Jersey Number: 3

Nickname: CP3

Hall of Fame: Still active

In a golden age of point guards, Chris Paul was at the top of the food chain. Then Steph Curry came along. Then James Harden emerged. Then Russell Westbrook. And Damian Lilliard. And Kyrie Irving.

Yet Paul is still there, and dangerous and lurking around that goal of winning an NBA title. He's still the scoring point guard and pesky perimeter defender who also happens to be the toughest player on his team. Four times he's led the league in assists. Six times he's led in steals. Twice he's averaged over 20 points per game. In those two years, he led the league in assists and steals both times. Paul is a coach's dream—an athletic point guard who runs the floor effortlessly, defends with tenacity, and shoots with proficiency.

When Paul was drafted fourth overall in the 2005 NBA Draft by the New Orleans Hornets, he made an immediate impact on his team and the state of point guards in the league. His rookie season, Paul led all rookies in points, steals, and assists per game, and became the second rookie ever to lead the entire league in steals. Within a couple of years, Paul had established himself as the NBA's premier point guard.

Fast-forward to today's game, where the point

guard position is now crowded with great players and yet an aging Paul is still among the cream of the crop. Sure, as of 2017, Paul hasn't yet taken his team to the NBA Finals, admittedly an even tougher feat in a Western Conference that looks like an All-Star Game every night. But he's shown that he might just have what it takes—in 2015, the Clippers didn't go all the way, but Paul fought hard in the first round of the playoffs, knocking out the defending champion Spurs in a tough seven-game series with a buzzer-beater off the glass. On the exciting Lob City Clippers, with dunkers Blake Griffin and DeAndre Jordan, Paul is the one who makes the engine go.

RUSSELL WESTBROOK
Years: 2008–present
Position: Shooting guard
Height: 6 ft. 3 in.
Team: Oklahoma City Thunder
Championships: 0
Most Valuable Player Awards: 0
Jersey Number: 0
Hall of Fame: Still active

For proof of just how different and athletic and amazing basketball has become, you need only watch Russell Westbrook, the electric point guard of the Oklahoma City Thunder. Westbrook plays the same position as Jerry West and Isiah Thomas and even Magic Johnson, but the NBA has never seen a point guard as athletic and explosive as Westbrook, who makes it a habit nightly to grab a defensive rebound, streak coast-to-coast, and throw down a massive dunk. Westbrook doesn't even need that much of a head start, for he could take a defender off the dribble, race past, and jam, even over much bigger guys.

It's the new game. Westbrook came out of UCLA in 2008, teaming up with Kevin Durant, another terrific scorer, and James Harden, whose attacking game gave the Thunder three of the best offensive players in basketball. Each player was special in his own way. The thin, six-foot-nine Durant was a sleek shooter with three-point range; Harden mastered the left-handed drive to the basket and the step-back three-pointer; and then there was Westbrook, so fast and physical, the power player as point guard.

With Westbrook at the helm, Oklahoma City

thundered through the Western Conference in the 2012 playoffs, advancing all the way to the Finals where they faced another deadly trio—LeBron James, Dwyane Wade, and Chris Bosh of the Miami Heat. The Thunder couldn't pull off the victory, facing one of the greatest teams in recent memory, but they showed they were the team to beat in the Western Conference.

Westbrook is so dynamic many basketball observers aren't even sure he is a point guard. Some say he is closer to the great Allen Iverson, whose scoring abilities were too valuable to have him worry about running the offense. During the 2014–15 season, Westbrook went where few point guards have ever gone, winning the NBA scoring title with an average of 28.1 points per game. Whether he scores with dunks, three-pointers, or fast-break points, Westbrook has made it known he is one of the most feared players in the NBA.

KEVIN DURANT
Years: 2007–present
Position: Power forward
Height: 6 ft. 9 in.

Teams: Seattle SuperSonics (2007–2008), Oklahoma
   City Thunder (2008–2016), Golden State War-
   riors (2016–present)
Championships: 0
Most Valuable Player Awards: 1 (2014)
Jersey Number: 35
Nickname: KD, the Durantula
Hall of Fame: Still active

For the hometown fans, there were many painful
aspects about the relocation of their beloved Seattle
SuperSonics to Oklahoma City, but one of the biggest
was having a player like Kevin Durant arrive from
the University of Texas at age nineteen, full of promise and championship potential, and only getting to
enjoy watching him play for one season.

When Durant, a six-nine forward who had the
wingspan of a seven-footer, entered the league,
with long legs and long arms on such a thin frame,
he looked like George Gervin, but with one exception: Gervin never had the range of Durant. Instead,
Durant had nearly unlimited range but in a forward's
body. In so many ways, Durant was another example of the modern game: the big player whose style

of play and unique skills really defied the makeup of conventional positions. In the old days, forwards weren't supposed to be able to shoot from that far away. But these weren't the old days, and Durant was a scorer that took the NBA by storm, winning the Rookie of the Year Award right out of the gate.

It wasn't just the points Durant scored, but how he produced them. Not only could he shoot from the outside, but he could also go inside and attack on the break or one-on-one. Though people concentrated on his range, Durant also led the NBA in free throws made for five straight years, proof that he was so difficult to guard he spent a lot of time at the foul line.

As Durant rose to the top of the league, fans began to wonder when the inevitable might occur, a championship matchup between the two greatest players in the NBA, Durant versus LeBron James. Durant led the league in points scored for five straight years from 2010–2014—averaging huge totals of 30.1, 27.7, 28.0, 28.1, and 32.0—just as James was establishing himself as one of the greatest players of all time. When they met in the 2012 NBA Finals, it felt like a prediction was coming true.

But James and Miami beat Durant's Oklahoma

City team in five quick games, and not only has Durant not gotten back to the Finals since, but also the competition has gotten stronger in the Western Conference and Durant's body has suffered serious injuries. Still, as long as his body is whole, Durant continues to be capable of greatness. He's already shown that he can defy the odds—many doubted whether this skinny, lanky, shoot-first forward would ever find his rhythm in the NBA. He proved the naysayers wrong and won his first league MVP in 2014. Paired with Russell Westbrook, the duo formed one of the most dangerous offensive combinations in the game. But now Durant has teamed up with Steph Curry, so the NBA can expect fireworks for years to come.

KAWHI LEONARD
Years: 2011–present
Position: Small forward
Height: 6 ft. 7 in.
Team: San Antonio Spurs
Championships: 1 (2014 Spurs)
Most Valuable Player Awards: 0
Jersey Number: 2

Nickname: The Claw

Hall of Fame: Still active

The dynasty already in place, Kawhi Leonard immediately became the face of the next chapter for the San Antonio Spurs. Like Steph Curry, Leonard wasn't the can't-miss Larry Bird, Michael Jordan prospect. He was a quiet kid from San Diego State University, not exactly a basketball powerhouse.

Leonard, though, let his skill on the court speak for itself. Playing for the Spurs, Leonard was not expected to lift the entire franchise. Tim Duncan, Tony Parker, and Manu Ginobili had already done that, but Leonard immediately started to impress his coach Gregg Popovich and the league with his hunger to improve and willingness to play defense.

Leonard, at six foot seven, can guard forwards and guards. He gained the nickname "The Claw" because of his ability to clamp down on defenders, even the best scorers (his battles with the most dynamic scorer in the game, Steph Curry, are already legendary). In those same matchups, he has also sent the message that he is a great offensive player himself.

Usually, players have to choose between being great offensively and defensively because doing both consumes so much energy. Only the greats can do both, and young Leonard has made it clear in a short time in the league he may be one of those players. After the Spurs' bitter loss to Miami in the 2013 NBA Finals, Leonard and San Antonio made it back in 2014, played Miami again, and crushed them in five games. It was Leonard, not the bigger names like Duncan, who was named playoffs MVP for his slashing offense and suffocating defense. The future is bright for this one.

THE PLAYERS OF THE 2010s
TOP TEN LIST

Once upon a time, the dunk was outlawed in college basketball. Illegal. You couldn't do it. Then, as a new class of highfliers entered the NBA, the dunk became as fun and as important as the game of basketball itself. Whether you bounce the ball off your head or dunk with style, it still only counts for two points. That doesn't mean that dunks aren't awesome to watch. Go to YouTube, and check out these masters of the dunk.

1. Julius Erving (Virginia Squires ABA, 1971–1973; New York Nets ABA, 1973–1976; Philadelphia 76ers, 1976–1987): Once dunked from the foul line. True story!
2. Michael Jordan (Chicago Bulls, 1984–1993,

1995–1998; Washington Wizards, 2001–2003): Air Jordan was Heir Jordan to the Doctor, following in Erving's flying footsteps.

3. Dominique Wilkins (Atlanta Hawks, 1982–1994; Los Angeles Clippers, 1994; Boston Celtics, 1994–1995; San Antonio Spurs, 1996–1997): The Human Highlight Film was especially known for his one-handed and two-handed windmill dunks.

4. Shawn Kemp (Seattle SuperSonics, 1989–1997; Cleveland Cavaliers, 1997–2000; Portland Trail Blazers, 2000–2002; Orlando Magic, 2002–2003): Power dunker from the 1990s.

5. Vince Carter (Toronto Raptors, 1998–2004; New Jersey Nets, 2004–2009; Orlando Magic, 2009–2010; Phoenix Suns, 2010–2011; Dallas Mavericks, 2011–2014; Memphis Grizzlies, 2014–present): His nickname isn't Half-Man/ Half-Amazing for nothing! His performance (and win) in the 2000 Slam Dunk Contest is one of the greatest ever—a must-watch.

6. Nate Robinson (New York Knicks, 2005–2010; Boston Celtics, 2010–2011; Oklahoma City

Thunder, 2011; Golden State Warriors, 2012; Chicago Bulls, 2012–2013; Denver Nuggets, 2013–2015; Los Angeles Clippers, 2015; New Orleans Pelicans, 2015): He's five nine and won the Slam Dunk Contest three times!

7. LeBron James (Cleveland Cavaliers, 2005–2010; Miami Heat, 2010–2014; Cleveland Cavaliers, 2014–present): One of the all-time great dunkers. Speed, power . . . everything.

8. Zack LaVine (Minnesota Timberwolves, 2014–present): A newcomer but an amazing dunker who won the 2015 and 2016 Slam Dunk Contests.

9. Clyde Drexler (Portland Trail Blazers, 1983–1995; Houston Rockets, 1995–1998): In college he jumped over five-foot-eleven-inch Andre Turner. Another true story!

10. Shaquille O'Neal (Orlando Magic, 1992–1996; Los Angeles Lakers, 1996–2004; Miami Heat, 2004–2008; Phoenix Suns, 2008–2009; Cleveland Cavaliers, 2009–2010; Boston Celtics, 2010–2011): Seven foot one, 350 pounds of pure power. He could dunk on anyone!

11. (BONUS!) Darryl Dawkins (Philadelphia 76ers, 1975–1982; New Jersey Nets, 1982–1987; Utah

Jazz, 1987; Detroit Pistons, 1987–1989): No list of dunkers is complete without Dawkins, who was known for his powerful dunks—so powerful that he shattered not one, but *two* backboards in 1979!

BONUS
TOP TEN LIST

ince there are too many to count, here are ten more of the best nicknames in the NBA!

1. The Black Mamba: Los Angeles Lakers great Kobe Bryant gave himself his nickname because, like the species of snake, he wanted to "strike with 99 percent accuracy at maximum speed, in rapid succession."

2. The Durantula: Oklahoma City forward Kevin Durant earned the nickname because he has lanky, long arms and legs just like a tarantula.

3. Big Shot Bob: Robert Horry, a journeyman who played on the Rockets, Suns, Lakers, and Spurs, was known for hitting the big shot with the game on the line.

4. Mr. Big Shot: Chauncey Billups, who played on seven different teams throughout his career, was

another player who reliably hit late-game shots in high-pressure situations, especially while playing for the Detroit Pistons.

5. Splash Brothers: Golden State sharpshooters Steph Curry and Klay Thompson are two of the best shooters in the league today—and two of the best ever. Night after night they "splash" the net with three-pointers. The nickname is also a nod to another pair of Bay Area teammates, Jose Canseco and Mark McGwire, who were called the "Bash Brothers" when they played baseball for the Oakland Athletics.

6. The Rifleman: Chuck Person, who played the bulk of his career for the Pacers and Spurs, was known as "The Rifleman" because of his precision three-point shooting ability and also because he was named after Chuck Connors, star of the old TV series *The Rifleman*.

7. Old Man Riverwalk: San Antonio Spurs future Hall of Famer Tim Duncan turned forty in 2016—combine the classic song "Old Man River" and the walkway that cuts through San Antonio, called the River Walk, and you have a name that

represents Tim Duncan's age and the city where he played.

8. Lob City: After the Los Angeles Clippers traded for point guard Chris Paul in 2011, teammate Blake Griffin, an impressive dunker, coined the term "Lob City" because he was excited about the prospect of Paul, a top-notch passer, throwing up alley-oops for him to slam in. Paul knows how to put 'em up, and Griffin sure does know how to throw 'em down.

9. The Truth: After Shaquille O'Neal and the Los Angeles Lakers defeated Paul Pierce and the Boston Celtics on March 13, 2001, despite the Celtics' loss, O'Neal was so impressed with Pierce's performance that he told a reporter, "I knew he could play, but I didn't know he could play like this. Paul Pierce is The Truth." Pierce's new nickname stuck.

10. Half-Man/Half-Amazing: After witnessing Raptors star Vince Carter put on one of the most mind-blowing performances in the history of the Slam Dunk Contest in 2000, Shaquille O'Neal (who was apparently as

good a nicknamer as he was a basketball player!), in awe of Carter's dunks, said Carter was "half-man, half-amazing." Seriously, you need to check out the highlights on YouTube!

THE FINALS OF THE 2010s

2010: Boston Celtics vs. Los Angeles Lakers

efore Game 1 of the Finals, the great Magic Johnson told Kobe Bryant that he was already a great Laker, one of the greatest players of all time for that matter. But Magic also told Kobe he had one more important task to accomplish in his illustrious career: all great Lakers have to beat the Celtics in the NBA Finals to secure their legacies.

This was not exactly true. Jerry West and Elgin Baylor and Wilt Chamberlain were all members of the Greatest Lakers Club, and none of them had ever beaten the Celtics for the championship. In fact, after years of Lakers losses to the Celtics, Magic had rewritten Lakers-Celtics history in the 1980s by beating the Celtics in two of three series. When Magic spoke to Kobe, he was really trying to provide just a little more motivation for Bryant. Bryant had unfinished business with Boston. The Celtics had humiliated the Lakers two years prior in the Game 6 clincher of the 2008 Finals, beating the Lakers 131–92 to win their seventeenth title.

A lot had changed in two years, though. The 2010 Lakers were already defending champions, having beaten Orlando the year before in six games. It had marked Bryant's first NBA title win without having Shaquille O'Neal as a teammate, equaling Shaq's feat in 2006 with the Heat, when the big man had won his only title without Kobe.

In the regular season, the Lakers won fifty-seven games, then raced through the playoffs and reached the Finals for the third straight year. For the second time in three years, they would play the Celtics.

And here they were again, the Celtics and Lakers, meeting for the twelfth time in history. The series was choppy, low-scoring, and bitter. Kobe scored 30 in the first game, but the Celtics stole Game 2 in Los Angeles with a chance to control the series. A breakout fourth quarter helped secure the win in Game 2, the Celtics lifted by Rajon Rondo's 10 points in the quarter. The young guard finished with a triple-double.

These Celtics were not exactly the same Celtics that had won the title in 2008. When Danny Ainge traded for Ray Allen and Kevin Garnett, the idea was to keep them together for two years. Now they'd played together for four and were in the championship again. Rajon Rondo, the fourth-year player who hadn't yet made a name for himself back in 2008, was now a star, and the only one of the core players whose career was still climbing. The Celtics looked old.

Boston won fifty games that season, but many of those victories had been a struggle. Few times during the season did their Big Four—Paul Pierce, Kevin Garnett, Ray Allen, and Rajon Rondo—click on the same nights. Game 3 of the Finals would be no different. With a chance to go up two games to one, the Celtics played one of their worst games of the series. Allen went 0 for 13 from the field, including 0 for 8 from three-point range. Kobe didn't shoot well, either—except when he had to. He took almost 30 shots (29 to be exact), and hit just 10 of them, including

1 for 7 from three-point range. Still, when you take nearly 30 shots in a game, you're going to pick up your share of points. He finished with 29, and the Lakers won 91–84.

LA was up 2-1 with two more away games left to play. Kobe improved his shooting accuracy in Game 4, going just under 50 percent from the field. He finished with 33 points, Gasol tacked on 21 more—but it wasn't enough. Not a single Celtic scored even twenty points, but it was a balanced effort, with important contributions from the bench, who scored 36 of the Celtics' 96 points in the victory. The final score was 96–89, Boston.

In Game 5, Kobe was even better, an offensive force who attempted to carry the team on his back. He finished with 38 points . . . and again, it wasn't enough. The Celtics core four got it done, Pierce leading the way with 27 points. Garnett finished with a double-double, 18 points and 10 rebounds, and the four stars combined for 75 total points. They edged out the Lakers 92–86.

Two close games, two Celtics wins. Boston brought the series back to LA, leading three games to two and needing just one to win the title. Despite being down to the Celtics, Bryant felt confident coming home, having combined for 71 points in the two losses.

That feeling intensified as Game 6 disappeared from the Celtics when starting center Kendrick Perkins injured his knee and was lost for the rest of the series. Boston had their core four, but Perkins had also played an invaluable role, especially on the defensive and rebounding fronts. Now he was gone, and suddenly, the Celtics had a huge void in their lineup.

The Lakers rolled by 22 points, setting up, yet again, a one-game-for-it-all showdown between Boston and Los Angeles.

The Celtics and Lakers had not played a Game 7 in Los Angeles since the famous 1969 Wilt-Russell battle, won by the Celtics. The Lakers hadn't played a seventh game in a Final series since 1988, when Magic and Kareem had won their last Showtime championship.

After a close first half, the Celtics took control of the game in the third quarter, amassing a 13-point lead. Was Boston's magic going to crush the Lakers all over again?

Father Time had other ideas.

Pierce, Allen, and Garnett had had their share of

injuries over their careers, and they showed their age in the fourth quarter. Pierce, no longer able to carry a team for a quarter by himself, wound up shooting 5 for 15. Ray Allen, suffering through a terrible period, shot 3 for 14, having been unable to find his deadly range all series. Kobe was no better, missing 18 of 24 shots, but he fought hard on defense and was tenacious on the boards (he finished with 15 rebounds). The Lakers chipped away and watched as the Celtics were unable to rebound or hit big shots while Derek Fisher and Metta World Peace came through on offense for Los Angeles.

The final score was 83–79, Lakers. They had beaten the Celtics and won the NBA title for the second straight year. Allen, one of the most accurate and prolific long-range shooters in NBA history, shot 36.7 percent in the series, 29 percent from three-point land, including 13 missed three-pointers in Game 3. Kobe was named Finals MVP for back-to-back seasons, and now had his fifth world championship over his career and second without Shaq. It was his last great moment.

Meanwhile, the Celtics' core four hung on for two more years. Overmatched by LeBron James and his new team, the Heat, the Celtics fought Miami but lost in the 2012 Eastern Conference finals before being broken up. Neither team would be championship caliber in the following years, but for one more season, the two elite dynasties in pro basketball sure put on a show.

2013: San Antonio Spurs vs. Miami Heat

This one had the feel of a throwback championship series like in the old days when almost every position on both teams was filled by a future Hall of Famer. San Antonio, already with four championships, boasted superstars Tim Duncan, Manu Ginobili, Tony Parker, and a young, budding talent, Kawhi Leonard. On Miami's side, there was LeBron James, Dwyane Wade, Chris Bosh, and now, having defected from Boston, Ray Allen. That's eight potential Hall of Fame players on one court to settle the NBA championship.

Quite a matchup it was. The Heat, now with LeBron James, had reached the Finals in the two years since his arrival, and in 2013, as defending NBA champions, did so again. James was the reigning NBA MVP and had won the award two years in a row. He'd also been named the Finals MVP the year before, but the Heat were not a one-man team. They also had Wade, and these two great players used their skills and basketball IQ to take over different parts of the game. LeBron had been the lone wolf in Cleveland, and it had been a while since Shaq had left Miami, meaning Wade had been the undisputed leader on the Heat for the past few years. It had taken some time for the two stars to learn to share the court, but they had finally begun to gel. With James and Wade at the center, Miami was full of excellent perennial All-Stars such as Allen and Bosh, as well as terrific role players like three-point shooters Mike Miller and James Jones. They looked like a team that would consistently compete for the title for years to come.

The Heat won sixty-six games in 2013, including twenty-seven in a row at one point. Wade suffered through injuries and wasn't the same player he had been, but he was still a dangerous force. James, still, was the engine. He was playing at the top of his power, always an imposing and unstoppable force when driving to the basket, but now dangerous from mid-range and outside. If James had mastered his jump shot and was already impossible to guard when his six-foot-eight, 250-pound frame drove to the basket, how could he be stopped?

Meeting the Spurs was something of a rematch. The Heat had never met San Antonio in the Finals, but James had, as a member of the Cavaliers in the 2007 Finals. The Spurs had destroyed Cleveland in four straight games, and now James, no longer an underdog, had unfinished business of his own with Tim Duncan, Manu Ginobili, and Tony Parker.

The teams split the first four games, but only the first matchup was actually competitive. In Game 1, James recorded a triple-double and was absolutely relentless rebounding the ball, finishing with 18. Yet he only scored 18 points, and Bosh and Wade had relatively quiet nights. Meanwhile, five members of the Spurs scored in the double digits, including a 21-point, 6-assist performance from Parker. Their team effort won the day as the Spurs defeated the Heat 92–88.

After that first game, hopes were high that each game would be just as tight. Yet the next three games were decided by 19, 36, and 16 points, with the Heat winning two out of three to even the series.

Then in Game 5, Danny Green, the Spurs'

three-point specialist, hit six three-pointers in a
114–104 win. That game showcased the masterful
efficiency of the San Antonio squad, one of the most
fundamentally sound teams in recent years. They
shot a remarkable 60 percent overall. The Spurs were
heading to Miami with a 3-2 lead, just a win away
from their fifth NBA title.

On Miami's home court, the Spurs led by 12 in
the third and by 10 entering the final quarter, 75–65,
but the Heat made a fierce comeback led by James,
who quickly scored 11 of the Heat's 20 points to start
the quarter. During that run, down 77–70, the Heat's
dead-eye three-point shooter Mike Miller had a shoe
come loose on the play, but he didn't have time to put
it back on as the play was still in progress. One shoe
was all he needed. LeBron passed the ball to him, and
Miller sunk a three.

Suddenly, the Heat led 84–82 with 6:03 left in the
game. Yet the Spurs were unimpressed. Smelling a
title, Parker and Ginobili turned up the heat, scoring
10 consecutive points to give the Spurs a 94–89 lead
with twenty-eight seconds left.

To match up with Cleveland's smaller lineup and
to keep the poor-shooting Duncan off the free-throw

line, Spurs coach Gregg Popovich removed him from the game. Duncan had scored 30 points through three quarters, but he was completely shut down in the fourth.

Twenty-eight seconds away for San Antonio. With a five-point lead, the Spur's victory seemed inevitable.

The clock ticked, ticked, ticked, shaving seconds off the clock.

Twenty-three seconds until James's season would end in disappointment if he didn't act fast.

Cleveland got the ball back and kicked it to LeBron, who fired a three and missed. But Miller was there to tap the rebound back to James, who launched another three-pointer. Good!

94–92, Spurs. San Antonio ball, twenty seconds left.

With 19.4 seconds left, Miller fouled Leonard. The rookie missed the first free throw but made the second, and extended the Spurs' lead to 95–92.

Miami brought the ball up, filled with a sense of desperation. With under ten seconds left, James fired up a game-tying three . . . no good!

The ball was up in the air, up for grabs . . . 6.3 seconds left.

Everyone scrambled.

Duncan watched from the bench. Bosh, the tallest man on the court, snared the rebound and tapped it into the corner for Allen, the man who had set the record for most threes in a season in 2005–06. Allen threw up one more three with five seconds left . . . it went in!

95-95, 5.2 seconds left on the clock. One more opportunity for San Antonio.

Parker missed a jumper at the buzzer.

Overtime.

The Spurs started out with another burst, rushing out to a 100–97 lead, but that was all the points they would score in overtime. They didn't score for the final 2:42 of overtime while James and Allen closed the deal. The final score was 103–100. The series was tied at three games apiece. It was a crushing blow for the Spurs, losing in what many consider to be one of the greatest NBA Finals games ever.

But there was still one more game to decide it all.

The series should have been over. The season should have ended with the Spurs holding the championship, up by five with twenty-eight seconds left in Game 6, but they had lost. Champions, however, fight. Champions recover.

The Spurs did fight, and they did recover in Game 7, but they did not win. Miami took the lead 72–71 to start the fourth quarter and fought off every charge. The Heat took the lead and held it. Leonard hit a three to cut the lead to 90–88, Cleveland, with two minutes left, but the Spurs would not score again.

James hit for 37 points, Wade for 23. The Heat won 95–88, and claimed their second straight title. After playing all those years for losing teams in Seattle and Milwaukee, Ray Allen now had two titles, one from Boston in 2008, and one in Miami.

How'd they do it? How did they win that Game 6 when it had seemed all but over?

Simple: they did what all coaches have hammered home since the dawn of sports—never give up and keep fighting until the very last second.

The Spurs never forgot. They tasted the bitterness of losing that title every day for the next year, every practice, every game, keeping the sour memory fresh in their minds in an effort to get back to the Finals. They did just that, and even crushed the Heat in a rematch that lasted but five games to reclaim the championship.

Weeks later, James left the Heat and returned to Cleveland, cutting short an era in Miami that many had thought would endure for years to come. But even in his brief stint with the Heat, James had taken Miami to four straight NBA Finals, the most consecutive Finals trips by any player since Bill Russell. A potential dynasty ended, but the NBA kept moving forward. Yet even as the years went by, the memory of the 2013 NBA Finals lived on, the lasting impact of a hallmark standoff between two of the greatest teams of the decade.

It's why, as basketball fans, we watch until the final buzzer sounds.

THE FINALS OF THE 2010s
TOP TEN LIST

Players change teams all the time. Getting traded or becoming a free agent is a normal part of being a professional athlete. But when the best players change teams, like when LeBron James left Cleveland in 2010 to "take his talents to South Beach" and play for the Heat, and then again in 2014 when he returned to Cleveland, the entire balance of the league shifts. Here are few instances when superstars departed for a new team in the prime of their careers and altered the league's power dynamics.

1. Kareem Abdul-Jabbar: As a member of the Milwaukee Bucks, Kareem won the 1971 title and reached the Finals again in 1974. Then he was traded to the Lakers in 1975, and Los Angeles

went on to win five NBA titles. Milwaukee hasn't reached the NBA Finals since.

2. LeBron James: Cleveland won sixty-one games with James in 2010. The next season, after LeBron signed with the Heat, the Cavs won just nineteen games. Meanwhile, the Heat won two titles and went to the Finals four straight years while LeBron was with the team.

3. LeBron James (yes, he's a *huge* game-changer!): After taking the Heat to four straight NBA Finals and winning two championships, LeBron returned to Cleveland in 2014. Having won only thirty-three games in the 2013–14 season, the Cavs went to the Finals in 2015 and won their first-ever championship in 2016. Miami, for its part, became an average team again.

4. Julius Erving: The New York Nets won the 1975–76 ABA championship while Erving was on the team. The next year, the Nets joined the NBA and Erving's contract was bought out by the 76ers—the Nets won just twenty-two games without him, the worst record in the league, and Erving took Philadelphia to the NBA Finals.

5. Wilt Chamberlain: The San Francisco Warriors reached the 1964 NBA Finals with Chamberlain at center, but after he was traded to the 76ers at the All-Star break the following season, the Warriors won just seventeen games. As a member of the 76ers, Wilt won the NBA title against his former team in 1967.

6. Wilt Chamberlain (another *epic* game-changer!): The 76ers won sixty-two games in the 1967–68 season, Chamberlain's last year with the team, before he moved on to the Lakers. By 1973, Chamberlain had been to the Finals four times in five seasons with Los Angeles, winning one title in 1972, while the 76ers won a pathetic nine (yes, nine!) games all year in 1972–73. It's still the worst regular season record in NBA history!

7. Moses Malone: Took Houston to the NBA Finals in 1981. Then he joined Philadelphia after the 1982 season and won the NBA title in 1983. Houston fell from grace and finished last place in the Western Conference the first two seasons after Malone went to the 76ers.

8. Charles Barkley: The 76ers were a playoff team until they traded Barkley to Phoenix. The Suns

reached the NBA Finals in Barkley's first year. The Sixers, on the other hand, wouldn't even reach the thirty-win mark in any of the next five seasons.

9. Shaquille O'Neal: With Shaq, Orlando went to the NBA Finals in 1995 and won sixty games the next year. Shaq signed with the Lakers in 1996 and later won three straight NBA titles from 2000–2002. The Magic were never as good after Shaq left the team.

10. Rick Barry: Helped lead the San Francisco Warriors to the NBA Finals in 1967, but he left the next year to play in the ABA. The Warriors weren't terrible in the years that followed, but they weren't championship contenders anymore . . . until Barry returned to the team in 1972. Barry and the Warriors would go on to win the championship in 1975.

11. Kevin Durant: In a move reminiscent of LeBron James' 2010 decision to form a powerhouse team in Miami, Durant shocked the league in 2016 and chose to join Steph Curry, Klay Thompson, and Draymond Green in Golden State to form a video game–esque squad of superstars.

EPILOGUE

THE REMATCH

2016: CLEVELAND CAVALIERS VS. GOLDEN STATE WARRIORS

How is it possible to have a classic, memorable, never-going-to-forget, all-time championship series when most of the games were so lop-sided? For instance, the winning team won each of the first six games by at least 11 points. Each team won a game by at least 30 points. One team, the defending champions, the Golden State Warriors, won three of the first four games and looked clearly superior to the other yet again.

Here's how: make the stakes so high for each team that every minute of every game is filled with so much pressure that the games don't even feel like games, but fierce battles.

Golden State against Cleveland, Round 2.

The stakes for the Warriors were enormous:

- They won a record seventy-three games, one more than the 1995–96 Chicago Bulls.
- They started the season 24-0.
- They finished 39-2 at home.
- They were the defending champions.
- Steph Curry was fresh off winning his second consecutive NBA Most Valuable Player Award.
- After four games, the Warriors had won three and were nearing a second straight title.

The stakes for Cleveland were equally large:

- The Cavaliers had never won an NBA title in their forty-six-year history.
- No sports team in the history of the city had won a championship since 1964.

- The Cavaliers had already lost to the Warriors the year before.
- LeBron James, though one of the all-time greats, entered the series with a 2-4 record in the NBA Finals.
- After four games, the Cavaliers looked done for. Dead, and buried.

By the end of Game 2, in which the Warriors destroyed the Cavaliers 110–77, on top of winning Game 1 by 15 points, it didn't even feel like this was going to be anything more than an easy walk to a second championship for the Warriors and another humiliation for James at the hands of Golden State.

After all, the Warriors had already overcome the hard part, which was beating Oklahoma City in the Western Conference Finals. Golden State had been down three games to one, with the clinching game being played on the Thunder's home court. The dream season looked doomed for the Warriors, but then Golden State showed the world once again their record-setting tenacity: Through a combination of toughness, heart, luck, and some key mistakes by the Thunder, the Warriors found a way to come back and win the final three games and the series. The Warriors were not only still alive, but they had just played two of their best games of the season. Heading into Game 3 of the NBA Finals, they had a five-game win streak going.

For James, humiliation was not too strong of a word. He had returned to Cleveland a year before to bring the city a long-awaited championship, but the Warriors had dashed his hopes—and that of an entire city who expected greatness—beating the Cavaliers by winning three straight games to end the series, having trailed two games to one after three contests.

During the regular season, the Warriors beat the Cavs on Christmas Day in a close game in Oakland. Later on, as Cleveland struggled during part of the regular season, Golden State came to Cleveland and handed the Cavaliers a loss so bad that they fired their coach, David Blatt.

Cleveland hired Tyronn Lue, a respected assistant coach, and made its march into the playoffs. They swept Detroit. They swept Atlanta. They beat Toronto in six games.

Now, in this Finals rematch, the Cavs were finally playing their best and with a full and healthy team, unlike during the 2015 Finals, when LeBron's co-stars Kyrie Irving and Kevin Love had both fallen to injury. Yet the Warriors mashed them by 15 and 33 points in the first two games and extended their winning streak over Cleveland to seven straight.

Game 3: If Cleveland loses, the series is essentially over. LeBron James knew this in his bones, telling reporters, "We can't afford to go down 3-0 to any team, especially a team that's 73-9 in the regular season and playing the type of basketball they're playing." On the brink of defeat, LeBron James and his fellow superstar teammate, point guard Kyrie Irving, launch an offensive attack against Golden State, scoring 62 combined points. Cleveland redeems itself, crushing the Warriors by 30, 120–90.

Game 4: Coming off of a brutal loss, the Warriors are up by two to start the fourth quarter. James and Irving try to mount a comeback, but the MVP Steph Curry, along with fellow Splash Brother Klay Thompson, rebuffs Cleveland's efforts, and the Warriors wind up winning by 11, 108–97, putting themselves a game away from the championship.

But the game ended on a bittersweet note for Golden State. After earlier issues in the playoffs,

Draymond Green, their emotional power forward, had been told by the NBA he would be suspended one game if he was involved in any altercation. Sure enough, during Game 4, Green got tangled up with James, leading to a confrontation. It was a short skirmish, but long enough for the NBA to suspend Green for Game 5 at home in Oakland, the potential championship-clinching game.

Before Game 5, the Warriors' fans taunted James, whom they thought used his influence as a star player to receive preferential treatment that had gotten Green suspended. They posted signs attacking James. Warriors players, such as sharpshooting Klay Thompson, also taunted LeBron, saying, "I thought this was a man's game" and "I guess he got his feelings hurt." Even Steph Curry's wife, Ayesha, got involved.

Maybe it was all too much for a player of such great ability and great pride. Maybe the combination of losing eight of the last nine games to Curry, losing his status as the league's MVP, and dreading the prospect of watching Curry and the Warriors celebrate another championship at his expense prompted what came next: one of the greatest responses in NBA history.

Facing elimination, James scored 41 points, grabbed 16 rebounds and dished out 7 assists in an upset 112–97 win. James was the best player on the court. He was unstoppable. Kyrie Irving, who for three of the first four games had appeared overwhelmed by the Finals, also scored 41 points, many of them with Curry guarding him. The season wasn't over yet. Cleveland was going home for Game 6.

A year earlier, the Warriors had won the championship in Game 6, at Cleveland. Not this time. Draymond Green was back, but it didn't matter. At the end of the first quarter, the Cavaliers led 31–11. James scored another 41 points with 8 rebounds and 11 assists. The Warriors, down 20 in the third quarter, cut the lead to nine, but would get no closer. In the final moments, Curry went for a layup. LeBron blocked it, looked at Curry, and taunted him. Ten seconds later, Curry was called for a foul, lost his cool, threw his mouthpiece, and was ejected. Suddenly, it was the Warriors, cool all year, better than everyone, who looked rattled. The Finals were coming down, improbably, to a winner-take-all Game 7.

How could this be? The Warriors had won so many games all season. Could the dream year actually be in jeopardy? Would the Warriors start the season 24-0, end it losing three games in a row, and become the first team in NBA history to lose the championship after leading three games to one? The previous teams with a 3-1 advantage were 32-0.

Game 7 was full of nerves. Neither team could break free. James didn't shoot well early. Neither did Curry. Tied at 89 with 2:50 left, the game, the championship, the season, came down to the final quarter, the final minutes. After a slew of blowout victories to begin the series, the fans watching the 2016 Finals would finally get the nail-biting storybook ending they'd longed for.

Both teams were swallowed up by the pressure. Veteran Warriors small forward/shooting guard and 2015 NBA Finals MVP Andre Iguodala drove for a layup, but he was denied when James made a spectacular block. In those final minutes, it seemed as though James was everywhere on the court. With 53 seconds left, Irving, guarded by Curry, nailed a fadeaway, off-balance three-pointer that gave Cleveland a 92–89 lead. Curry, who had hit so many magical shots all season, worked and worked for an opening, before ultimately missing a long three. In the final seconds,

James went in for the clinching slam dunk, but was fouled by Green. James made one of two foul shots to put the Cavs up by four, 93–89.

It was over. Cleveland, at long last, had its championship. James had beaten Curry, the Warriors, and all the doubters. Irving had proven himself a championship player. James crumpled to the ground and cried, overcome with the emotions of all he'd been through. He finished with 27 points, 11 rebounds, 11 assists, a triple-double. He was named Finals MVP. He had been challenged to be the best player in the league at a time when the world seemed more focused on the young upstart, Steph Curry. But James had vowed to bring a championship back to his hometown, and against the most improbable of odds, he delivered.

In 2016, the King still reigned.

A TIMELINE OF BASKETBALL'S KEY MOMENTS

(TOP 40 STYLE)

1. 1946–47: The Philadelphia Warriors win the first Basketball Association of America (BAA) Championship. The league is renamed the National Basketball Association (NBA) three years later.

2. 1949: The Minneapolis Lakers win the first of two consecutive championships and five over the next six years, which included the first time a team won three championships in a row in NBA history (from 1952 to 1954).

3. 1955: The twenty-four-second shot clock is implemented.

4. 1956: St. Louis Hawks Hall of Fame forward-center Bob Pettit is named the inaugural winner of the NBA Most Valuable Player Award.

5. 1957: Led by rookie Bill Russell, the Boston Celtics win their first NBA championship. They would go on to win many more—Boston's seventeen total championships is the most of any franchise in NBA history.

6. 1962: March 2: Wilt Chamberlain scores 100 points in a 169–147 win over the New York Knicks in Hershey, Pennsylvania, the most ever in a single game.

7. 1962: Wilt averages an NBA record 50.4 points per game, scoring more than 50 points in forty-five games throughout the season.

8. 1962: Oscar Robertson becomes the first (and only) player ever to average a triple-double throughout a full season (30.8 points, 12.5 rebounds, 11.4 assists per game).

9. 1962: Elgin Baylor scores an NBA Finals record 61 points in Game 5 of the championship series at Boston.

10. 1966: The Boston Celtics beat the Los Angeles Lakers to win their eighth straight NBA championship, a record across all professional sports and one that may never be broken.

11. 1966: Legendary Celtics coach Red Auerbach

names Bill Russell his successor, making Russell the first African American head coach in American team sports history.

12. 1967: The 76ers win sixty-eight games, a record at the time that has since been broken. Chamberlain beats Russell for the first time in a playoff series. The 76ers beat San Francisco for Chamberlain's first NBA championship.

13. 1967: The American Basketball Association (ABA) is founded as a rival league to the NBA.

14. 1969: Bill Russell wins his eleventh championship in thirteen years, the most all time by a single player, as Boston defeats the Lakers in seven games. Russell retires.

15. 1972: The Lakers win a record thirty-three straight games and their first NBA title in Los Angeles after seven tries.

16. 1973: The 76ers lose a record seventy-three games . . . just six years after they set the record for the most wins in a season!

17. 1974: Moses Malone joins the ABA, becoming the first player in history to join a professional team directly from high school.

18. 1976: The ABA folds. ABA teams including the Indiana Pacers, Denver Nuggets, New York Nets, and San Antonio Spurs join the NBA.

19. 1976: The Boston Celtics and Phoenix Suns square off in an epic Game 5 of the NBA Finals, with Boston winning 128–126 in triple overtime! It was the longest Finals game ever and arguably the most exciting game of all time.

20. 1979: Larry Bird and Magic Johnson join the NBA, ushering in a new era of NBA popularity.

21. 1979: The three-point line is introduced in the NBA.

22. 1980: Magic and the Lakers beat the 76ers in six games for the NBA title, the first of five titles in the 1980s.

23. 1981: Bird and the Celtics win the NBA title in six games, the first of three titles in the decade.

24. 1984: Kareem Abdul-Jabbar becomes the NBA's all-time leading scorer on April 5 in a game against the Utah Jazz. He would eventually retire with 38,387 total points, a record that still stands today.

25. 1986: Michael Jordan scores a playoff record 63 points in Game 2 of the first round of the playoffs at Boston in a 135–131 Chicago loss.

26. 1992: Despite having retired due to contracting the HIV virus, Magic Johnson is voted a starter in the All-Star Game and is named MVP.

27. 1992: The US Olympic team that included Michael Jordan, Magic Johnson, Charles Barkley, and Larry Bird, nicknamed "The Dream Team," wins the gold medal.

28. 1995: John Stockton surpasses Magic Johnson as the NBA's all-time leader in assists in a game against the Denver Nuggets on February 1. He would finish with 15,806 total assists in his career and still remains the all-time leader today.

29. 1995: In his fifth game back in the NBA after taking a year off to play professional baseball, Michael Jordan returns with a vengeance, scoring 55 points against the Knicks at Madison Square Garden on March 28.

30. 1996: The Chicago Bulls win a record seventy-two regular season games—a record that would be broken two decades later. More on that to come.

31. 1996: Kobe Bryant joins the NBA directly from high school, paving the way for a slew of highly talented high school players who would later enter the NBA Draft, including Tracy McGrady, Dwight Howard, and LeBron James.

32. 1998: The Chicago Bulls win their sixth NBA title, with Michael Jordan hitting the final game-winning shot. Jordan is named the Finals MVP for the sixth time and announces his retirement after the series ends.

33. 2000: Shaquille O'Neal joins Kobe Bryant with the Lakers and Los Angeles wins the first of three consecutive NBA titles.

34. 2003: Straight from high school, LeBron James makes his NBA debut with the Cleveland Cavaliers.

35. 2006: In a January 22 matchup against the Toronto Raptors, Kobe Bryant drops 81 points, the most ever since Wilt Chamberlain's 100-point performance.

36. 2008: The Boston Celtics win their first NBA title in twenty-two years, defeating the Lakers in six games.

37. 2011: James leaves Cleveland for the Miami Heat, beginning a stretch of four straight NBA Finals appearances and two titles.

38. 2014: The Spurs defeat Miami for their fifth NBA championship and the fifth for Tim Duncan.

39. 2014: LeBron returns to Cleveland. The Golden State Warriors beat Cleveland to win the NBA championship for the first time in forty years, and begin the 2016 season 24-0.

40. 2016: The Golden State Warriors win seventy-three games, the most all-time in a single season, beating the Jordan-era Chicago Bulls' former record of seventy-two wins. The San Antonio Spurs win sixty-seven games, making it the first time in league history that two teams finished with sixty-seven plus wins in the same season. But wait, we're not done just yet! On the same night the Warriors win their seventy-third victory, in the final game of his career, Lakers legend Kobe Bryant goes out in style, scoring 60 points, the most ever in a career finale, on a record 50 field goal attempts. And that's not even the biggest milestone, which would

come in the final game of the season. Cleveland
would become the first team in NBA history
to overcome a 3-1 deficit in the Finals, shocking
Golden State in seven games, and becoming
the first Cleveland sports team to win a
championship since the Cleveland Browns
in 1964.

INDEX